The Ca

Runni_g

To my jovial shipmates without whom none of the voyages would have taken place.

The Call of the Running Tide

Wallace Clark

(with a little help from his friends)

Edited by Bruce Clark and Tara Mackie

 Rathlin Island Books

First published in 2012 by Rathlin Island Books.

Distributed by Rathlin Island Books.

RIB #02

Cover art: original painting of *Wild Goose*, Copyright © Finn Clark, 2010.
Painting of Fingal's Cave, Copyright © Ros Harvey, 2009.
'Sea Fever' is reprinted with the permission of The Society of Authors as the literary
representatives of the estate of John Masefield.
The extract from the Irish Cruising Club obituary is reprinted with the kind
permission of WM Nixon/ICC.
'The Nine Lives of *Wild Goose*' and 'Lessons of a Lifetime's Cruising' are reprinted
with the kind permission of Yachting Monthly.
Back cover photograph by Mike Tinne.
Inside sketches by Fiona Barber, except the semaphore sketch by Robin Cole.

ISBN: 978-0-9568942-1-2

Printed by Impact Printing, Ballycastle, Co Antrim (www.impact-printing.co.uk).

Rathlin Island Books
4 Church Bay, Rathlin Island, Co Antrim, Northern Ireland, BT54 6SA.
www.rathlinislandbooks.com

Contents

Acknowledgements

During the last few years of life, Wallace felt an overwhelming urge to put together a book that would encompass the entire range of his seafaring. He wanted to crystallise his own memories, and also to impart to future generations the excitement of life on the waves during a period when sailing underwent a revolution.

Any list of those who, directly and indirectly, made it possible for Wallace's final literary ambition to be realised would be very long indeed. We should begin by thanking those who helped adorn this book with pictures that highlight every phase of Wallace's life at sea. We share Wallace's deep appreciation of the work done by Finn Clark on the cover. We also thank Sarah and Jill Clark for taking trouble to find and send family photographs; Charlotte Laurain for digitising photos supplied by her father Mike Tinne; Ann Henderson for digitising slides; Alistair Jameson for his wonderful curragh photos; Kelly Allen for her photograph of *Wild Goose* sinking; Johnny Scott-Barber for allowing us to use drawings by his mother Fiona Barber; and Ros Harvey for offering a beautiful painting. Thanks also to Winkie Nixon for penning a very thoughtful obituary.

Both editors consider themselves very lucky to have collaborated with Stephen Ryan and Jessica Bates of Rathlin Island Books: a superbly professional publishing duo who entered deeply into the spirit of this unusual book and have coaxed us along with exemplary efficiency, calmness and humour.

By the time Wallace suffered a serious road accident in November 2010, he had completed most but not all of the necessary editorial work. When Tara took over as editor in 2009, she was building on foundations laid by Louisa Porritt and other helpers. In all his later writings, Wallace relied on his dear friend Beverley Scott for word-processing and on Gavin Hill for computer wizardry.

The friends and family who helped finish this book, after Wallace's death on 8 May 2011, are all members of that wide-ranging and colourful fraternity of people who played some role in his maritime life. They were asked to contribute because they could throw light on particular episodes in his long maritime career, and all responded with warmth and enthusiasm. But Wallace's sailing fraternity was, of course, much wider. To mention only a handful of names, any list of seafaring companions would also include Dubliners like Lewis and Melanie Purser, James Osborne, and the late Paul Campbell. There would also be Scottish highlanders and islanders like Ranald MacDonald and his son Andrew; Alistair and Sheena Scott from Skye; Michael Gilkes from Islay; and the fishermen, crofters and lairds who welcomed Wallace to every one of the Western Isles. Donegal friends like Lynn Temple would feature on the list, as would Ulstermen like Ricky Butler, Sir Dennis Faulkner and Robin Dixon, now

Lord Glentoran. There would be hospitable Sassenachs from the RCC such as Christopher Thornhill and his family, Libby Purves, and the London-Irishman, Judge Andrew Phelan. In his final years, Wallace was also lucky enough to acquire a whole new set of Connaught-based sailing friends through the Frères de la Côte (Brotherhood of the Coast), including John Coyle and Sean O'Loughlin. Des Moran was his guide in all west of Ireland matters, social and maritime.

Wallace's final six months in hospital seemed, at first, like an almost terminal blow to any prospect of finishing this book successfully. But in an uncanny way, his hospital stay was turned to good effect. Both the editors were able to have long bedside chats about his memories of sailing, and his hopes for the book. He corresponded about the book with his grandson Finn, and asked him for a cover illustration; Finn's offering was duly approved. Both Finn and his sister Georgie supported their grandfather with loving and encouraging cards. Among the people who sustained him in hospital through visits, correspondence and prayers, his sailing friends loomed large; and they all, in different ways, helped to keep him alive for a few crucial months and hence helped make this volume possible. Commander Peter Campbell, a Rathlin man, was a devoted visitor and has been a vital supporter of this book. Mike Tinne, a shipmate from the 1940s to the 2010s, accompanied and sustained Wallace on his final days on earth, as did Heather Simpson (and her children) and Valerie Henderson. Only days before his death, Wallace had a long, rich conversation with Ian Harvey, a journalist with deep family roots in Malin; they talked in astonishing detail about boats, bays and islands. Sally Liya (nee Villiers-Stuart) was a kind and practical visitor to the Royal Victoria Hospital; she and Wallace reminisced about her sea-dog father Mike. Jane Mackie boosted Wallace's literary hopes by presenting a copy of her own superbly-edited memoirs. Eveleigh Brownlow and cousin James Leslie encouraged him with news of the RNLI, a cause to which they were all devoted. If Wallace had any peace of mind on his bed of pain, it was because he knew that dedicated helpers like Peggy O'Kane and Mary O'Donnell as well as sister-in-law Kay Deane were looking after his wife June. And as his final voyage loomed, he was also very well supported in matters of the spirit. As well as the Maghera clergy, Isaac Hanna and Mark Lennox, and the chaplaincy of the Royal Victoria Hospital, and his old friend Dean Cecil Orr, Wallace received prayerful succour from Canon Jonathan Barry, whose late father Canon John Barry had co-organised the curragh voyage in 1963. The Barrys, *père et fils*, had always been admirers of Wallace's seafaring talents, and in return they shared with him their wisdom in eternal matters. It seems very fitting that this book begins with a vivid, well-told story from the funeral address delivered by the younger Canon Barry on 13 May, 2011 at St Lurach's Church.

'I hope to see my Pilot face to face
When I have crost the bar.'
(Tennyson)

Introduction

...the dragon-green, the luminous, the dark, the serpent-haunted sea, the snow-besprinkled wine of earth... (James Elroy Flecker, Gates of Damascus)

My father Wallace had a keen and mysterious intimacy with the ocean. He was brought up near the flat dams of a mid-Ulster linen village, and schooled on the River Severn near the English-Welsh border. But from the beginning he yearned for wider waters. His parents Harry and Sybil excelled at many things, including golf and gardening, but neither was a sailor. Yet Wallace always wanted to master the waves. He had a mild phobia of being under water for more than a few seconds, but scudding over the salt sea, in calm waters or rough, simply felt like the most natural thing in the world: a place he was called to be. Not just in big ships commanded by other people, but in small vessels of his own.

After two years' service in the Royal Navy, and a season's adventure on a cattle ship bound for South Africa, he settled down to work in the family business, and the need for maritime escapes became more intense than ever. At a time when cruising round the north and west coasts of Ireland hardly existed as a pastime, he taught himself to sail, and started picking up a huge treasury of knowledge about the geography and local lore of the Irish and Scottish coasts. He also developed a set of instincts about tides, winds and waves which would stand him in good stead in more distant waters, those of Brittany, Norway, the Mediterranean and ultimately exotic places like the Azores and Cape Horn.

Reading these reminiscences by Wallace himself as well as his crew, friends and family, it should be possible to understand a little more clearly what the sea meant to him. Northern Ireland in the early 1950s was a deeply conservative, rule-bound place, where distinctions of class and religion were rigorously observed. He was called by birth to a modest place in the Northern Irish establishment, and the family business which he joined was an august institution, rather top-heavy with family members. To a degree that must have frustrated an energetic and imaginative young man, the scope for individual initiative or wild, spontaneous behaviour was limited. The sea was his liberation. It was a habitat for which he had a natural affinity, a world where he instinctively knew what to do, and could inspire complete trust among his crew and companions.

Nobody who sails in a small boat can ever be pompous, he used to say. As he discovered, people who lived near the sea or from the sea – be they fishermen, lifeboat-men or old naval salts – formed a seamless community where he won instant acceptance. Seafarers of all stripes took him to their heart. They recognised him as one of their own. Although his giant frame was not especially graceful in its terrestrial movements, and he was no ball-room dancer, Wallace could manoeuvre a boat through stormy seas with a waltzer's grace. That was one of the observations made by Canon Jonathan Barry, in the first of four reflections by Wallace's life-long sailing companions...

BRUCE CLARK, May 2012.

Reflections

Rev Canon Dr Jonathan Barry
St Lurach's Church, Maghera, 13 May 2011

How fortunate a man I am! I remember with great clarity the moment, as a young lad of 13, I first met Wallace. It was on Downings pier, Co Donegal. It was, I believe, the summer of 1960. And *Wild Goose* was alongside.

It was a late afternoon in August, the sky was darkening, the wind rising in the nor'-west, gusting 5-6, a rain squall sweeping in across Sheephaven. Somebody in the family cottage overlooking Sheephaven saw there was a boat coming in. Well out to sea, there was indeed a yacht, storming along. My father and I took turns with the binoculars, watching. In time it became clear she was heading for Downings. On she came, white water foaming at the bow, the port side well under at times. And on the stern was a man the glasses showed clearly, a strong man, great shoulders, cradling the tiller, moving with the rhythm of the boat. Watching through the glasses my father suddenly said – and I do not make this up – "I've got to meet that man! Come on!"

We were standing on the pier by the time the boat arrived. She swept across the end of the harbour wall at a thrilling pace. Suddenly she turned hard to starboard, up into the wind. I expected the sails to drop, and the motor to take over. But no, with great noise and shaking of rigging, she came about until, with wind on the port quarter, heeling hard over to starboard, she headed straight for the shore, parallel to the harbour wall.

I did not expect what came next. About three lengths out from the harbour wall, that tall man, half crouched in the stern, glancing at the berth where I stood, shouted his command to the crew. The helm went hard over, round she came, once more, to point almost head to wind and right at the wall at my feet. The sound of the wind in the sails I will never forget. Dramatically she slowed, and easing away, came to a halt, the fender kissing the stone. A young man, early twenties perhaps, stepped easily ashore, and in one fluent movement had her tied at the bow. The giant of a man on the stern meanwhile had tossed a rope to my father, who quickly obeyed his command and lashed it to a bollard. *Wild Goose* was secure.

Billy Patterson

I have always thought of Wallace Clark as a Viking – an out of time and place Viking. That was my first impression when I met him first in 1963, when he was in his thirties and I was but a lad of twenty-one. But that was because of his Nordic features – the strong jaw, deep-set eyes and unruly hair, also the love of adventure, the mischievous humour, the fearless spirit, the good companion. Although he was an Ulsterman through and through, I never changed my opinion of him. I will always remember him as a Viking.

In my subsequent friendship with him I discovered that this was a Viking who loved poetry, had a good heart, deep feelings for his family, a caring concern for his shipmates, an interest in the lives of others. He was essentially a very kind man. I am also very glad that I never had reason to cross him in all those years, as his wrath could be backed up by a commanding physical presence and an unblinking glare which made one glad that one was in his camp, and usually resulted in a peaceful end to little problems.

Back in 1963, I was lucky to be chosen as one of the 13 crew of the Iona curragh of which Wallace was the skipper. I met him first when I was called as first reserve to the shores of Dundrum Bay in County Down where we were to have a training run in the recently completed 30-foot long curragh. It was a choppy day and my reservations about going out in a flimsy craft of wood and tarred calico were allayed by the presence of the skipper who inspired confidence in his relatively inexperienced crew, and by the presence of the builder of the curragh, Jim Boyd, from Bunbeg. Several of the crew were Church of Ireland ministers including the man whose idea it was to re-enact the voyage of St Columba from Derry to Iona – Canon John Barry, but all of us were sailors or oarsmen and had some experience of being on the sea.

It really was choppy and became choppier as the morning progressed. The curragh twisted alarmingly as bow and stern met different forces, but that was alright. Wallace was there with a smile and a crack, pulling his oar like the rest of us. We rowed three 14-foot oars each side with a man in the stern working the steering oar.

While I was rowing I was fine, but when I had to sit in the bottom of the lurching boat for several interminable periods, my stomach gave up the unequal struggle, and I remember hanging over the gunwhale looking at the cattle in the distant fields and would willingly have changed lives with any of them.

It was my first experience of sea-sickness, but thankfully just about my last. I was never afraid, just sea-sick, but on reflection I seem to recall *sotto voce* mutterings from the clergy which may have been calls for heavenly assistance, or they might just have been asking themselves (like the rest of us) what the blazes they were doing there!

With great relief all round we gained the shore and discovered that the calico had come adrift on the transom and was only an inch or two above the water-line. We dragged her up and slept in an empty fish factory which despite a strong smell seemed like the Dundrum Hilton to me. I remember we spliced the mainbrace that evening and Wallace entertained us with a few of his less bawdy songs and poems due to the presence of the gentlemen of the cloth. I should add that they were all great chaps and not at all prudish, but one respected their vocation.

The actual voyage itself in June 1963 was almost an anticlimax after that training run. We had only light winds and relatively calm seas, but alas could not use our primitive rectangular sail as this type of vessel can only use wind power when the wind is coming from a point astern. As it came from the northeast for the duration and we were heading nor-norwest, we rowed all the way. The only real danger came from bullets fired by soldiers on the range at Magilligan as we skirted that shore. We heard the whiz and plops as they passed overhead and fell in the water.

Wallace usually sat in the stern with the steering oar, his charts and a small radio with which to contact the *Tor of Moyle*, our support vessel. He got his leg pulled about his lack of effort as we were doing all the rowing – 14 hours straight from Port Ballantrae to Lossit Bay on western Islay – and to which he always had an appropriate response, and, anyway, no one minded really as he was the skipper and importantly also in charge of the rum rations, the dispensation of which usually started when the 'sun was over the yardarm'. On the longer stretches of open water the first one to spot land got a tot and my young eyes usually enhanced my rum ration.

On the island of Mull when we had time in hand, some of us went out for a short run on the *Tor of Moyle*, a converted fishing boat, and as we approached the shore we were entertained by Wallace, buck-naked and waving a towel back and forth in front of him and running crab-like across the sand in a bad imitation of Gipsy Rose Lee.

We had time to visit Fingal's Cave on Staffa on a relatively calm day, and while in its cathedral-like interior were inspired to give the Hallelujah Chorus a quick airing, followed by Wallace stripping off, quickly joined by the rest of us, and all diving into the gentle but brooding swell.

Many memories I will treasure from the Iona Voyage, but I believe my favourite was sitting around the campfire at night on the soft sand of a deserted Hebridean island, chatting, singing, telling yarns, a few smoking, tots of rum all round – a wonderful feeling of companionship and camaraderie as we listened to the crackle of the sticks and stared into the heart of the fire, smelled the wood smoke and listened to Wallace's soft cultured tones speak of many things.

Shortly after the Iona Voyage, Wallace enlisted my help to bring *Wild Goose* around the coast and into Mulroy Bay along with his brother, Henry (if memory serves me right). They sailed the boat, we all had several tots, I made the tea, and as night fell was prevailed upon to repeat my not inconsiderable repertoire of doubtful stories to a very appreciative, if small, audience. Next thing I knew Wallace says, "Right, we're off to bed. Steer for that light, then that light and when you're abeam it give me a shout," and the two lads disappeared below. I sat there with the tiller in my hand never having sailed a boat in my life, but it can't be too hard I thought, if they trust me to do this. There was quite a wind from the north and I was steering west, the gunwhale was in the water and my heart was in my mouth – but I managed to follow the complicated instructions! It was getting light when I called Wallace, who took over, swung the *Goose* into Mulroy Bay and promptly ran up on a sandbank.

Since then I helped row and sail the *Aileach*, a replica Highland galley, around the west of Ireland with Wallace again at the helm, or, more accurately, the steering board. On that trip his son Miles was the action man, camera and notebook in hand as I ferried him ashore in the inflatable so that he could photograph the galley from a high vantage point on the mainland. Another Viking was young Miles, a chip off the old block; an author like his Dad, a sailor and adventurer like his Dad – but we were not to know then that he did not share the confidence we had in him.

After Miles died and *Wild Goose* was still in the Black Sea, Wallace brought her back home in 'legs'. I did the La Coruna in Spain to Newlyn in Cornwall leg with him and Tony Harvey his Australian friend. This trip included a couple of visits to naval museums in Spain where Wallace seemed to be known, which did not surprise me.

Everywhere I have ever been with him, from remote islands off the coast of Ireland to grand houses with titled people, and in Spain, people either knew him or knew of him, and he was always warmly greeted.

Once again we were lucky with the weather crossing the Bay of Biscay, and on that long, slow voyage I believe I got to know Wallace – the inner man – very well. In the middle of the night with the gentle flap of the sail and the quiet drone of the little engine we shared confidences and spoke of things that can only be shared with true friends, and I was pleased to be considered so. He spoke of his love for June, his sadness about Miles, his love for and pride in his son Bruce, and his grandchildren.

He roped me into becoming a 'Frère de la Côte'; I flew him to Mull; we had several curragh re-unions over the years in Gorteade Cottage and Ardtara; he recorded a programme with me for Highland Radio; I launched Ros Harvey's and Wallace's book at Greencastle; he gave me a bed for the night, I gave him a bed for the night; he came to my theatrical productions in Letterkenny; I brought him in my boat around the southwest coast of Ireland – and in these things our lives intertwined over the years.

I am not one who is easily impressed, but Wallace Clark did it on the day I met him and that never changed. He was my hero and my friend. I miss him.

John Fishbourne

My first sail with Wallace Clark on his beloved *Wild Goose* was on a stormy early October day in 1963. He had lent *Wild Goose* for the summer to naval friends at HMS *Sea Eagle*, Londonderry and wanted her back in Portrush before winter. He himself had spent the year helping to recreate the heroic voyage of Columba when the saint and 11 monks rowed a curragh from Derry to the Isle of Iona and founded the monastery there, 1,400 years earlier. He helped and advised on the building of a modern replica of the ancient craft and after a service of blessing at the cathedral in Derry, he skippered the vessel to Iona, where in turn they were met by the then Archbishop of Canterbury, the moderator of the Church of Scotland and many other dignitaries. Next year, incredibly, will be the 50th anniversary of that epic adventure.

I met Wallace and his golden Labrador Ben, midmorning on a very blustery day in October on the quay in Derry, half expecting the trip to be cancelled because of high winds and a dubious forecast. Wallace was also not pleased with *Wild Goose's* condition – the radio wasn't working, and nor was the engine. I murmured my regrets but Wallace was not to be put off. "It doesn't matter at all. There is a strong ebb tide and a favourable wind, we don't need the motor. We will be in Portrush before dusk. So jump aboard!" Sails were hoisted and we set off down river as fast as *Wild Goose* ever went. It crossed my mind that if either dog or crew fell overboard we would have been left to swim ashore. But as neither the dog nor Wallace seemed at all nervous I put all negative thoughts away. We had an exciting sail in Force 6 or 7 and got to Portrush without trouble – crewman and dog still aboard.

This was the start of many sailing trips with Wallace and June over the next 30 years in the Hebrides, the west of Ireland, in the Med, in Brittany, the Greek isles, Turkey, the West Indies, and across the Bay of Biscay to Spain – either in *Wild Goose* or a variety of charters. Wallace always had a yarn about any place we visited and knew the history and customs of everywhere we went. After my first brief sail to Portrush I would cheerfully have sailed with him anywhere or everywhere in any weather condition. He was not only a very fine seaman, he was also a life-enhancing companion, full of ideas and with a huge interest in the maritime history of these islands, and was himself a most talented author of many books.

On one of our many cruises in the Hebrides, I remember dancing Scottish reels at night in a farmhouse kitchen in South Uist with the head of the Clan MacDonald and his family. Wallace's friendship with the MacDonalds furthered his interest in the maritime history of the 'Lord of the Isles' kingdom – and eventually this led to the building of a replica galley – the *Aileach* – in which they sailed and rowed, in a heroic voyage in 1991, from the west of Ireland to the Scottish Islands. Later the galley went as far as the Faeroes. An earlier voyage to the Hebrides with Wallace and his son Miles, and my son John, ended with a wonderful day's deer-stalking on Jura.

Life with Wallace was always fun, full of high adventure, never dull. He is sadly missed.

Joy McCormick

The Ponderosa Bar stands quite alone on the Glenshane Pass, Northern Ireland's highest pass between east and west. A chance meeting there led to a lifelong friendship. Donegal-based Liam McCormick, my future husband, was driving home westwards when he suddenly saw, parked on a trailer, a fine craft unknown to him. It was called *Wild Goose*. It took only seconds for him to park up, enter the bar and encounter the owner, Wallace Clark.

Liam, an architect, had just completed several voyages to Scandinavia in his Donegal built boat. Wallace, a linen man, had just sailed around Ireland and written a book about it. Quickly discovering that they were both members of the Irish Cruising Club they swapped reminiscences of the sort of sailing adventures usual to ICC members. A major spark in their relationship was the realisation that both their sailing grounds were close to each other – along the northwest coastline of the country.

They became the lords of the coastline between the mouth of the River Bann and the Magilligan Straits at the mouth of Lough Foyle, with too many passages to remember or record. Our family home was there on the Greencastle shoreline. Its little port below the house was too small for *Wild Goose* so Wallace usually moored on the Grey Horse Rock just outside. We never knew when he might appear there, usually with a crew full of interesting friends. Men who I meet nowadays often remind me that they have been in our home!

And then, of course, there were longer trips such as a fabled one to the Morbihan in France. This had such an emotional effect on Liam that he insisted in taking me to that part of France to propose marriage! June, Wallace's wife, I'm delighted to say, was usually with us on these trips back then. She was someone whose seamanship I admired a lot, but even more to admire was her composure under stress and her good looks. In bitter east winds and storms, June remained calm and beautiful on deck, while I cowered below.

And so began many years of sailing companionship, often sailing together in their mutual area of coast. Some trips were more serious, such as rounding Inishtrahull in strong winds and tides. Others could be a little saunter along the coast. These could become quite unexpectedly dramatic, such as a submarine suddenly surfacing quite near to us in our comparatively small boat at the

Foyle mouth. We were a bit shaken at its closeness, when out of the conning tower lined up six sailors who stood at full salute while the captain assisted an obviously very senior officer along the deck to board a tug from Derry which had just come alongside. The tug then turned to return up the Foyle Estuary. The submarine began to submerge, and then, mysteriously, to rise again. The tug returned, the submarine's crew lined up again on deck and a bright pink hot water bottle was seen to pass between them to the tug crew, before the submarine submerged once more to gales of laughter from our boat!

The friendship went beyond Ireland and the sea. Both men were visitors to the Royal Thames Yacht Club in Knightsbridge, a handy place to stay when in London, and lots of entertaining was done there. There was a lighter side to their friendship. In 1975, when commissioned to build a Catholic church in Maghera – just miles from Wallace's home – Liam said teasingly that he was building an unusually high tower so that Catholic bells might be heard in Upperlands for the first time!

Back on the water, the Lord of the Isles Voyage was conceived and carried out by Wallace and his crew close to our home. On his many visits to Greencastle he had become well known in the locality. So when it came to the Galley, he had it constructed by three men in McDonald's Boatyard (1760). A 'homely sort of man', one of them called him. And he was well liked in the community. This was reflected at the launch in Moville, when one of the three took him on his back and managed to tip him into the water. The friendly laughs and cheers from the shore expressed the people's affection and respect for him.

After many adventures, the Galley called in to Greencastle in 1991. It was at least 10pm when a neighbour rang us from the point to say it was on its way to us. Remembering that there was no sleeping accommodation onboard, I hastily made up every spare bed and sofa in the house. Kevin O'Leary, the American cook onboard, had a small thatched cottage locally where three or four stayed. It was terrific having the rest of the crew here, until the realisation dawned that these strong men would need a substantial breakfast! Our son was dispatched to an out of hours' supplier promptly!

Following Liam's sad death in 1996, Wallace continued to sail this way, at first by boat and later by the new ferry which runs from Magilligan to Greencastle. June, who sadly by then was housebound, kindly allowed me to accompany Wallace to various events such as an annual dinner of the ICC in Limavady.

What I really want to do someday is to stop at the Ponderosa Bar with a family friend to thank Wallace's spirit for the many happy and interesting encounters that Liam and I had with and through him. He was a great man to know and friend to have.

CHAPTER 1
Fugitive Brothers

Bruce:

Wallace's closest childhood playmate, during his early experiments in sailing and other activities, was his brother Henry, who in later life made his mark as a politician, Africa hand and oarsman. As this chapter makes clear, Wallace also liked his Clark cousins, so numerous they formed a cricket team. But as a brother only two and a half years his junior, who shared the same mixture of governesses, boarding schools, and rough-and-tumble of life in a country area where petrol was short, Henry was Wallace's first and main companion.

Henry died in March 2012, having outlived Wallace by barely ten months. In the days before his death, Henry was hard at work on a contribution to this book. In a touching token of the two brothers' closeness, Henry tried to write in Wallace's voice as he described their shared adventures. Here are a few lines penned by Henry but in what he imagined as his brother's voice...

Henry writes as Wallace:

Quite often people ask me how I learned to be the skipper of a yacht. Why did people enjoy sailing with me? Then, answering their own questions, people would say: "You're a reliable seaman and take few risks; you chat to everyone and never boss or scold." That is a nice sort of compliment. Looking back I see that my experience as a leader was built up over a number of years, from the time my brother and I both had bicycles. Henry seemed to accept my leadership as first among equals. At first, our expeditions were simply to tea and tennis with our many cousins. Collecting birds' eggs led to some more exciting trips... like scrambling up to a heron's nest wearing climbing irons. Later the trips got even more thrilling... for example when we found a small cliff face in the Sperrin mountains on which both a raven and a peregrine falcon had laid eggs on a very small ledge and we had to climb down with ropes. Doing these things together made Henry and me into a natural team, or on a boat, a natural crew.

Wallace in his own voice:

My brother Henry and I learned to row a boat and trim sails on the tree-ringed dams in Upperlands, County Derry. There were also minor expeditions between the bushy banks of the Clady River, which only had enough water to float us during a flood. There the biggest hazard was getting the mainsail caught up in overhanging pine branches. When so stuck, there might be attacks by our three piratically minded Clark cousins, Roddy, Desmond and David, who would seize our good ship, *Falcon*, and carry us off as prisoners to tea at Upperlands House.

There were also occasional voyages through the green countryside down the River Bann. But as schoolboys we were never allowed to follow the river to the point where it entered the North Channel through the sand hills near Portstewart. The sea, in our minds, was invested – perhaps infested – with sudden gales and huge breakers rising out of calm water. Our father was away at the War and our mother was right to be cautious.

Three years later we were on the lookout for our first sea-going vessel. *Fugitive* was acquired when I returned from England aged 23 as the lowest form of animal life afloat – a midshipman, Royal Naval Volunteer Reserve. A three-ton cruising yacht, 18 feet on the waterline and designed by Milne, *Fugitive* was to be our first decked boat. She was a middle-aged lady, a relic of an early Belfast Lough No 2 Racing Class and cost us the princely sum of £100. Someone had put a deck over the forward cockpit – a real cabin for the first time and my pride and joy!

Henry and I sailed *Fugitive* from Whitehouse on Belfast Lough coastwise to the wee box of Carnlough harbour, and slept the night on shelves in her four-foot high cabin. It was a big deal for us. We were independent ship owners, afloat and cruising at last!

The next day a kindly south wind blew us north through Rathlin Sound to Portrush. Johnny Doherty, most kindly of harbour masters, found us a place to lay the mooring. Fees would be… wait for it… £3 per annum! Once we had her secured we slid into our dinghy, *Imshi* (a rudish version of 'Go away!'), and rowed ashore. Stepping out at The Old Dock we almost staggered like real sailors. We were deep water men, by God! Luckily, there was no one around to watch us as we walked up to the Royal Portrush Golf Club to get a lift home with our parents, who had been much relieved to spot us sailing past an hour earlier.

At the weekend *Fugitive* took us to Bunagee Pier, a mile north of Culdaff, just to show off to our cousin Olive who owns the sand hills behind the glorious beach; she came down the river in her own mini power boat to see us. *Fugitive* had a curved, two-foot high bow, but less than 12 inches freeboard aft. There lay her weakness. In bad weather offshore she would be bound to take a lot of water on deck, and if it found its way below would be hard to keep afloat. We made a note to avoid being caught out.

Next call was Tory Island, seven miles offshore, just short of the Bloody Foreland. After an overnight passage we arrived mid-morning on a Monday, around the time an Irish island likes to wake up. A man from East Town took our head rope with the apology, "I haff no English." Gaelic, said to be the purest in Ireland, was spoken by all Tory people in 1950. It was then, and remains, the most isolated Irish island community, with around 100 uninhibited inhabitants.

The Dixon family of four unmarried brothers; Hughie, Johnnie, Jimmy, Denis, and sister Grace, took us in for warmth and hot drinks. The District Nurse repeated the treatment. The Parish Priest, all 20 stone of him, came out to bless the boat in our tiny canvas dinghy. The islanders' familiarity with their curraghs gave them undue confidence in the dinghy's real capacity! Later, the Father asked us in for a dram, pouring whiskey out as if it was beer.

We were shown round the mile-long island, including the Wishing Stone and, with more care, the Cursing Stone, which was said to have brought about the wreck of HMS *Wasp* when it came out to collect taxes. To get a wish you had to stand on an isolated pinnacle on top of the red north cliffs and throw a pebble out to land on another pinnacle, ten feet away. Having had no sleep the night before, I missed, but beginner's luck brought what I had wished for – a gentle west wind to blow us back home. Later onboard that night, Jimmy Dixon brought out a six-foot grapnel to add to our tiny anchor. We went to sleep feeling secure, while a fleet of small curraghs paddled past us to fish off the western point – a nightly occurrence.

We visited Tory regularly after that, and the Dixons became great friends. I used to wear rouge Breton fisherman's trousers long before such things became popular in London sports stores. This made me known on the island as 'the man in the red trousers'. Derek Hill, the painter, used to have a hut there and depicted some breath-taking scenes. And thanks to him, Jimmy Dixon became a well-known primitive artist.

*****

One Friday night in July, Gordon Clark and I felt elated as we looked forward to a fortnight's exploratory sailing westwards. At 0930 the next morning James Henshall, a Belfast Lough yachtsman, joined us. At 1000 we slipped, bound for Killybegs, 120 miles away, and the west coast after that.

By 1100 the 'Gas Buoy' off the entrance to Lough Foyle was abeam. The southwest wind which had given a comfortable broad reach began to veer and pipe up more strongly. We already had one reef down and soon gave up the idea of rounding Malin Head that day. Closing up to the coast for a lee and pushed along by the flood tide, we were able to drop the pick at lunchtime off Bunagee Pier, Culdaff. This is the loveliest of all the bays in Donegal. On this northeast coast of Inishowen, green vegetation clothes the 200-foot cliffs down to the water edge. Only at Culdaff is the pattern broken by a mile-long stretch of bright golden strand and a shallow river mouth. Behind that rises the gaunt cone of Slieve Snaght. It is often a cloud maker and on that day grey wisps streamed off its head, a sign of breaking weather.

On the west side of the bay Croagh Glengad climbs steeply to its rounded summit. Its sides are a patchwork of tiny fields and white cottages. This is a perfect setting for an anchorage, albeit an exposed one. If the wind comes in from the east you have to get out double quick. Alongside the pier at high water we were welcomed by Denis Munigal, a tall raw-boned figure who lived with his sister, Madge, and brother, Willie, in a white cottage nearby. He knew every tide, counter tide, rip and overfall on the coast which he has fished off in engineless boats all his life. Very good he was too at explaining to us their locations. In the evening he told us stories of cod fishing in January when the baited lines had to be de-frosted with boiling water before eight men crews set out to row nine miles to Eighteranova Bank. Coming in with the catch, sometimes almost gunwhale deep, they would make it a race because the first boat in got the best price from dealers on the beach.

Our cousin, Olive Young, was kind enough to let James sleep, shower and shampoo in the Salmon House. Beside it stood the Watch House where until 1920 Coastguards kept a look out for smugglers. Mostly ex naval men, they would sally out in their big cutter with scrubbed white sails to board suspicious shipping. Lying off the beach we went to sleep to the sibilant whisper of a swell which seemed to tell of slithery sea snakes, singing sirens, syllabubs, shindigs and the moans and mews of the sea. *Fugitive* was turned beam on to the swell by the ebb from the river, and rolled heavily all night. It seemed to us a long one.

The next day the wind was a strong southwesterly so we explored the Eskalon Cave, trying to hook a conger eel, and then the cave under Dunmore Head where you can see an 18-pound cannon ball lodged in the east wall. It was fired by a frigate as a demonstration for Robin Young, the Laird a century ago. At six in the evening the wind dropped and a light air from the east tempted us to try for the Head again. But as soon as we got to Carrickawaddy (The Dog Rock) it turned west, strong and gusty. Turning back we had a perfect reach in calm water, the silver grey deck gleaming in the half-light and our bow wave bright with phosphorescence. Cottage lights twinkled on the shore as we anchored off Bunagee at midnight. "You were better back," said Denis in the morning. "Malin Head is a cross wee spot."

On a third try the next day with a light variable wind we sailed at 1400 and were close to Garvan Sound by 1700 in a flat calm. Out came the trusty Seagull Outboard to be clamped on the starboard beam to help dodge the sunken rocks through which the tide runs fiercely in confusing eddies. An hour took us past The Shoulder, the apt local name for Ireland's north point and another hour round the west of Malin itself. What a disappointingly low extremity it is for a country that has such magnificent cliffs elsewhere.

By daylight we were within the wide arms of Lough Swilly ten miles south. Bacon and eggs for a second breakfast tasted especially good alongside the pier at Portsalon. Friends were staying in the hotel and Mary, my cousin Billy's wife, came out for a sail. Later we dined ashore in luxury.

That night at near high water we tucked in close to the pier in what seemed a snug position. What I had failed to learn from the Irish Coast Pilot is that the tide which drops six feet at Portrush and four at Ballycastle, drops nearly 14 here. Within two hours we were bumping on sand that seemed as hard as concrete; it was too late to pull out into deeper water. There followed one of the most comfortless and worrying nights I have ever spent in a boat. The banging seemed hard enough to break the old ship to pieces. If that did not finish us off and we failed to find enough ropes to hold her tight in to the pier, she could well heel over against it when dry and break her mast against the stones. Bang! Whump! Crunch! Scrape! It seemed enough to shake your back teeth out. How could any vessel stand up to it? I had no previous experience to judge by, but managed to scramble onto the pier and dash up to the hotel to see if we could borrow anything to act as fenders or planks to steady her. "Nothing available," was the answer. Not even sympathy. The owner-manager was no sailor and went grumpily off to bed.

At last the water fell right away and the bouncing stopped. Gordon and I got a couple of hours' sleep. Then as the water rose it started again worse than ever. When she finally floated we took an anchor out in the dinghy with our last warp and with a 'Heeya Hiya Hulla Hulla Haul!' manoeuvred her into deep water. The wind was blowing quite strong onto that accursed pier by now, but we seemed to be holding. James came out to join us and we sailed off to shelter in Macamish Bay. He told us that the manager had remarked, "The silly young boy in the yacht didn't know what he was doing." Perhaps he was right. All our worries seemed to have been unnecessary, however. *Fugitive*, stronger than she looked, made no more water than usual and seemed to have suffered only a few deep scratches along her topsides.

Swilly, known as The Lake of The Shadows, is full of niches for a small boat to explore – Scraggy Bay, Fort Lenan, Fahan Creek, Ramelton River and more. We spent a pleasant week poking our nose into each of them. Wildfowl in thousands were feeding on the mudflats on each side of the Channel as we returned, including the last of the hordes of overwintering Brent and Barnacle geese. We had a picnic supper at Macamish in the Martello Tower which contains a furnace for heating Red Hot Shot. Knockalla and Dunree Forts were two other interesting landings. They seemed to have been established, like so many War Office projects, long after any risk of the French landing had gone. They came into their own, however, at the beginning of World War I when squadrons of battleships from the Grand Fleet unexpectedly used Swilly as a refuge from U-boats.

We decided to return home overland – the Brown family on Inch Island lent us a mooring and would keep an eye on *Fugitive* until we returned. The last thing we did before we left was to feast on a boiling of crabs gathered from holes in the rock off Ballymastocker Beach. The Swilly is a fun place to cruise in.

Now Henry, once again writing in the voice of Wallace, describes a voyage they made to Mulroy Bay:

I t was July 1950 before I could set out on another cruise with my brother Henry, who was captain of boats at Trinity College Dublin. Trinity's tour of Irish Regattas had just ended. They had won the Rowing Union's 'Big Pot' at New Ross. This meant they had been acknowledged as the fastest eight in Ireland for the second year running. As for me, I was working in the family linen business and got the week of 12 July as a holiday. We decided to explore Mulroy Bay in Donegal. Not far away from home, but a piece of water neither of us had sailed into before. From Portrush we headed west round Malin Head and anchored for the night in Lough Swilly in the shelter of the Martello Tower on the western shore. As we found next morning, the mouth of Mulroy was only about five miles further but we turned into it with relief, as a westerly wind was blowing small waves over our stern, finding the leaks which had been left unrepaired. Like several other sea loughs of north Donegal, Mulroy has a broad unimpressive entrance. The coast pilot warned that after about three miles it narrowed suddenly. This was the point where, depending on the tide, sea water flowed into the fresh water of the upper lough, or else water flowed out. As so often, the dangers which the pilot warned of proved less than we had feared. With the outboard running we motored through without any problem, even though the so-called Third Narrows, at a point known as the Hassans, were very narrow indeed.

Once we passed that point, we were inside the upper lough, and the scenery changed immediately. Its shores are well wooded and the water is very clear, though full of hundreds of large jellyfish, which fortunately did not seem to sting when we went for a swim. From the Hassans, we sailed north, keeping quite close to the land. There was a green wooded island, with what looked like a holiday shelter – about the only sign of life we were to see. (The small town of Milford is close to the southern end of the lough, though not actually on the shore.) We found a friendly bay at the north end where we anchored for the night. On that first voyage, the whole lough had all the charm of the unexplored. Little did we guess that Mulroy would later become a favourite base for family holidays.

On the second day we sailed south again. It was warm and sunny when we anchored in the upper lough, so we hung out most of the damp bedding to dry. Then after climbing into the dinghy we set off to visit a farm that we could see at some distance, in the hope of buying milk. As almost always happens in those parts, we were immediately made welcome. Payment for refilling our milk bottles was declined and we ended with half a dozen eggs for our tea. When we walked back to shore, we were worried at first because we couldn't see our boat in the place where we had anchored her. Then we looked round a corner and realised that with blankets hoisted up to dry, the little ship had dragged her anchor. Catching up with her in the dinghy was no problem... and we sailed back to anchor close to Hassans Pass, ready to head home the next day. At an early stage in our return, we decided to turn into the small fishing port of Downings near the mouth of Mulroy.

One reason for stopping there was to ring home and let everyone know that we were *safe. When my brother Henry took the phone, our father told him a letter had come from the colonial office which offered him a post as a district officer cadet in Tanganyika. This was the good news Henry had been hoping for but made success in his final exams in October all the more important.*

We got back to Portrush quite late that evening and enjoyed a family toast to the colonial service. It had been a short, rewarding voyage of exploration which we had both enjoyed. Sadly if my brother Henry was to be in Africa, there might not be chances of many more.

CHAPTER 2
Escaping the Flax Mill

Bruce:

*A*s we have already seen, most of Wallace's early sailing on the north coast of *Ireland was in small boats of which he was the proud owner and skipper. But this log describes a voyage in those waters with his cousin Roland, the only one of his Clark kin who was a keen enough mariner to have a sea-going boat of his own. (It probably helped that Roland's father and namesake was a decorated naval commander, who had sadly died very young.) This log describes a period when like Wallace, Roland was learning the textile trade in Belfast; and just like Wallace, Roland was straining at the leash, yearning for an open-air life where he was his own master. Roland later acted on that impulse by emigrating to New Zealand, where he became a successful farmer and journalist. But Wallace and Roland remained in very close touch and they exchanged many visits. In the weeks before his death, Wallace often dreamed that he was revisiting Roland (who had died in 2004) and they were exploring the loughs and glaciers of New Zealand.*

This log is introduced by Roland's daughter Bee Dawson, who is herself an accomplished writer on subjects ranging from gardening to the New Zealand air force.

Bee begins:

*O*n a gloriously sunny August day in 2010 I stood with Wallace on Horn *Head in Donegal overlooking the sweeping expanse of Sheephaven. Wallace was still in fair health, although this was only a few months before he suffered his ultimately fatal accident. The heather was in purple bloom, the sun shone, the sands and cottages were startlingly white against the surrounding green, I was marveling at the loveliness of it all when Wallace suddenly pointed across the bay and said: "Over there, that's where your father Roland and I sailed in, early one morning in 1949. We'd sailed all night, right around from Portrush, and berthed at Downings, in time for breakfast." It was quite extraordinary to have my father's presence so beautifully and unexpectedly evoked.*

Even after 46 years in New Zealand my father Roland Clark always described his cousin Wallace as his first and very best friend. Those early years spent in and around the Clark family houses and linen mill in County Derry or mucking around in boats off the Ulster coast were never forgotten. Whenever Dad reminisced of sailing adventures to Irish islands and quaint little Donegal ports he would colourfully recall the fishermen's curraghs, thatched cottages and the friendliness of everyone they met as they nursed a fortifying pint of Guinness at the end of a day. It was hardly surprising that these two adventuring cousins got on so well. Not only did they share many of the same passions (family history, sailing and the taking up of life's challenges), but they both had a warm and abiding interest in people, irrespective of their social class or occupation. They were also natural communicators who were renowned for their ability to write and talk at entertaining length – I suspect that neither of them ever allowed veracity to get in the way of a good story!

That day on Horn Head I was highly impressed that Wallace could recall this early voyage so clearly. What I didn't know, of course, was that Wallace had been working on his log books, translating the entries into a book in his inimitable style, ensuring that even a 61 year old adventure was as fresh in his mind as if it had happened the previous summer. It is wonderful that it is now published for the enjoyment of all. Let's raise a celebratory glass to Wallace and Roland: adventurous spirits, colourful communicators and intensely loyal friends.

Wallace:

The first cruise I ever made started on the north coast of Ireland on a fine Friday evening in July 1949. It was the postwar period when holidays seemed short in length and few in number. But 'The Twelfth' was a weekend when marching took place in most parts of Ulster, and employers gave the Monday and Tuesday off for revellers to sober up.

My cousin, Roland, and I, both recently de-mobilised from the Royal Naval Reserve, were in Belfast serving our time as apprentices to the city's linen trade. Our 18-foot half decker lay on a mooring in Portrush Harbour. Her name, *San Ferian*, came from the French phrase, *Ca ne fait rien*, 'it doesn't matter' or 'never mind' – and such an appropriate name as we rushed out of work early that day without a backward glance, impatient to get to sea. The train that brought us from Belfast reached 'The Port' at 1830 hours on the Friday evening. Friday is supposed to be an unlucky day to go to sea, but most of my voyages have started on Fridays to maximise time after work. We do not seem to have been jinxed yet.

San Ferian was as keen to get to sea as we were, and seemed to give a roll and a wink as we walked from the station past her mooring in the roomy artificial harbour. A colossal supper followed at Roland's house from the hands of Norah, my favourite aunt. Then Roland's brother, Dick, arrived in his Jeep to help load blankets, ground sheets, jars of water, cans of fuel, a primus cooker, foodstuff, tools, oilskins, torches, donkey jackets, binoculars and a pair of coastal charts.

Davy Wilson, taciturn but helpful, let us use the private jetty where he kept his 'Boats for Hire' beside the Lifeboat House. As I sculled *San Ferian* alongside, the sea air was like a tonic simultaneously cooling my cheeks and soothing a throat rough from flax dust. The gut-ripping prospect of four days ahead to explore a coastline we hardly knew was like pennies from heaven.

The sky was clear, the glass high and the wind was a light northerly. Stubbington, the strict old Excise man and a retired Naval Petty Officer, came along to give us clearance since the sail to Donegal would mean crossing an international boundary. Then at 2200 hours, at low water just as the flood tide started to run west, our mooring buoy dropped over the bow with a satisfying 'plop'.

At 2230 hours, with our course set west-northwest, 25 miles for Inishtrahull Sound, and southerly winds forecast, the wind died as the sky darkened. We shipped the outboard on the starboard beam and it started with a fine roar, driving us forward at a speed of nearly four knots. By 2300 hours we decided to set three hour watches and Roland turned in beside the centreboard case. I refilled the outboard tank at midnight with the lights of Lough Foyle broad on the port bow, and two hours later the Inishtrahull Light was on our starboard bow, seven miles away. Roland surfaced and took the tiller, and with the tide still running west with the boat, steered past the three Garvan Islands as it was too dark to risk the passage inside them.

Just after 0400 hours an undistinguished bulge of bare rock – Ireland's North Point – lay abeam. The gables of cottages dotted along the shoreline began to show brilliant white and the pattern of field walls around them sharp black in the dawn sunshine.

At 0445 hours we rounded the Scart Rocks off the west side of Malin in a swirl of meeting tides. Before us stretched the three great bays of Swilly, Mulroy and Sheephaven, with Tory Island, Inishbofin and the Bloody Foreland just beyond – all inviting exploration, all offering friendship and shelter, and all within a few hours sail. This is the vista I came to know so well later and named 'The Yachtsman's Finest View of Ireland.'

By 0730 hours we were alongside Downings Pier. A 50 mile passage under ten hours – aided by the main tidal streams and luck with 'counters' running inshore. An irate Belfast man complained we were blocking his berth. "We are not. Hell roast you!" said Roland, knowing just how to deal with awkward complainers. But for peace, we moved off later and lay to anchor.

Peter Larmour, Roland's fellow apprentice in Jennymount Mill, Belfast, had told us he would be in a tent beside the pier. Roland was determined to let said tent down on top of him just to prove that we had made it. Peter had not believed we would. (Nor had we!) There was only one tent in sight so we prepared to flatten it but luckily, just before slackening off the guys, found that Larmour was not inside it. End of raiding party. After the long night watches, Roland almost got his nose wet as he fell asleep over the soup. I only just avoided doing the same. However, the food revived us so we took our hosts for a sail later, picnicking in wooded Monk's Bay and swimming off the sweeping beauty of Marble Strand, a couple of miles west of Downings.

On our return we met the McNutt family at the base of the pier. They were most kind and plied us with more soup, sandwiches and, best of all, a room ashore with two beds at their house called Nutville with the promise of a shower in the morning. Before we turned in for the evening, however, we needed to work on the boat. The lower pintle of San Ferian's rudder had worked itself loose on the passage across the previous night so we beached her on the rising tide and wading around her, removed the rudder. A local garage kindly welded on to it a six-inch base plate which we screwed securely into place.

The next morning, seen off by Peter Larmour, we slipped away from the pier for home. By mid-morning we were anchored in Pincher Bay, just inside the Fanad Light, to await a fair tide round Malin Head. We examined six local curraghs, an ideal vessel for local fishing, but the crudest build on the coast – the 'ribs' are withies with the bark still on, tied into place with spun yarn. The skin covering is of any old cotton, heavily tarred. They need to be re-ribbed and skinned every three years.

A painter working on the lighthouse gave us two crabs which we boiled in a bucket along with some spuds. With the mackerel we had managed to catch on spinners that morning, they made a fine lunch. By 1600 hours, after creeping round Ireland's North Point again, we turned inshore and tied up at Portmore Pier. "Hullo, men," said a figure above us. "Tie up wherever ye like." Then the figure offered us a lift to get petrol for our jerry can.

Still flat calm, the decision was made to try for Inishtrahull for the night, Ireland's most northerly island, seven miles northeast. We slipped out between the Garvan Islands and the twin humps of Saddle Rock, and just as we cleared them a fog patch reduced visibility to 50 yards. After a moment's consternation we found that the foghorn on 'The Hull' (Inishtrahull) was giving us a course to steer – the only snag being that the exhaust from the outboard thundering against our topside was so magnified by the fog that it made it impossible to hear each blast! We proceeded, however, stopping the engine every 20 minutes to listen for the horn. We also checked our ex RAF Grid Compass to make sure we were steering off enough to compensate for the three-knot cross-tide. Some vessel, probably a motorised fishing boat, passed us at speed 100 yards ahead, unseen. Our faculties, so sharply attuned that we could have heard grass growing by that stage, had me down below in a trice, rummaging for a tin tray which we could bang as an improvised signal as to our existence. After several listening stops, we made out a pale grey hump ahead. As we got closer, we saw a figure standing on the rocks pointing east. He looked like The Metal Man who shows the way into Sligo. We assumed he must be an alert light keeper as he followed us along the shore as we proceeded towards the end of the land.

Inishtrahull showed on our chart as a blunt arrowhead pointing west, a mile long, with hills at each end rising 100 feet. There must be a few flat acres in the middle and, above all, the chart shows a natural harbour around the corner. The east projection showed an area clear of rocks so we double closed round it. A colony of friendly seals with pups eyed us from Gull Island. Tilted spars appeared looking like a crane. "That must be the pier," said Roland. We chugged on westward through a whirlpool which forced our head round towards the Black Rock. It was quite a fight back to maintain course as the outboard on the beam made turning to starboard very slow.

Portmore, the natural harbour opened up at last. The figure who had guided us reappeared, somewhat breathless. "I'm the PK," he said (Principal Keeper). "We were sure you were a damaged seaplane trying to taxi in."

Our little four Horse Power engine must have positively chuckled with delight at this. The extraordinary power of fog to amplify sound has never since been better demonstrated. We thanked the keeper for his pilotage and handed up a can of beer. "Yon's a happy goose," he said, "None of that's kept here." Other light keepers appeared and, once over their surprise, were most hospitable. "Will yous come over to the Light for a cup of tea?" "Sure will," Roland replied.

The keepers of the Horn at the west end all insisted we visit them first. We solved the problem by having tea with each in turn. We were shown the 12-foot stone column at the west end bearing a resemblance to the Virgin with a child in her arms. We bowed our heads and said 'a wee mouthful of prayer' in thanks for our safe arrival at this unique place of worship. It was a half circle of boulders against the rock, on the south side of a hillock. A cross roughly inscribed made a flat stone serve as the altar. This was the sole relic of Christian worship and led to a conclusion that a Viking raid around 900 AD had killed or carried off as galley slaves the whole population. 'The Hull', as it is known, was inhabited sporadically in the 18th and 19th centuries, but was finally evacuated in 1929.

Back at the lighthouse we were invited for supper. The table had a recess containing a saucepan of cooked potatoes at one end. Each of us was invited to help ourselves and take our pick from a pile of mackerel caught from the small green boat we had seen in the port. At the back of the handsome stone building stood three separate dwellings, relics of heroic days when wives accompanied their men folk to live on the island. The west end PK telephoned on the line linking the two ends to offer us beds in a spare room where later the mighty blasts of the horn made the walls tremble and seemed near to shaking us off the mattress. But after a few minutes we learned to sleep through it. At about 0400 hours the fog lifted and we missed the 'Noises Off'.

The port showed up as a rocky creek, 70 yards long with a short jetty near its head. Not a ripple disturbed its surface and oyster catchers probed the mud at the head with long red bills. Eider ducks with their half-grown families swam in and out. A solitary heron circled overhead. Wheatears, my favourite of all maritime birds, flashed their pinky breasts and white rumps among the rocks and terns squawked and flapped as we approached their nesting place. The colouring would have pleased Cézanne – blue sky with puffy clouds, the sparkle of a cerulean sea and amaranthine shadows as tawny seaweed draped the granite rocks with green grassland aglow above.

Six hours of fair tide and puffs of north wind carried us homewards past humpbacked Glengad Head on which tradition says the last wolf in Donegal was killed in 'a Sheugh on the Croagh'. There were friendly waves from a Culdaff boat hauling pots on Eighteranova Bank, then came the mile of golden Magilligan Strand, fringed with a narrow strip of white surf. By 2200 hours we were moored in Portrush again among the Uffa Fox 18-foot Nationals, which race often but rarely go cruising. Then, what Roland called the riskiest passage of the weekend, getting from *San Ferian* to the Old Dock in his seven-foot six clinker tender, *Impshi*. We disposed of that hopelessly short dinghy soon afterwards and got a Prout folding flattie with a canvas bottom and plywood sides, which did years of good service.

Many a weekend cruise we made in later years in other craft, but never a better one than that first run to Downings. It gave life to the saying, 'The smaller the boat, the bigger the adventure.'

We got to know Inishtrahull well over the following years, and the welcomes of the light keepers were always genial. The most famous light keeper, D J O'Sullivan, studied the island wildlife and wrote a column about it in the 'Irish Times'. He included, one year, the arrival of a snowy owl that preyed on the island's rabbits and on another occasion described the sex life of a pair of insects he had in a matchbox in his pocket.

Once all ships could fix their position by radar, a foghorn was no longer necessary. So manning was reduced to one crew for the Light. A new steel tower for it was erected in 1965, and the splendid old stone building on the east abandoned. In the late 1980s, the Light became automatic, requiring only maintenance visits. 'The Hull' is a much duller place without the keepers, but its natural harbour, little used and rarely rough in summer, is a super place for yachts to call in to. And Carr Rock, a mile northwest of 'The Hull', is also worth a visit. It is a great place for lobster potting.

The hospitality and kindness of the McNutt family in Downings became a family byword. We remain forever grateful for the way they dried us out on this occasion and after several other sodden arrivals.

CHAPTER 3
Fisherman's Regatta

Bruce:

*I*t is often said of Wallace that he was almost exclusively a cruising sailor: he did very little racing. But this statement has to be qualified. He crewed on a Belfast-based 15-tonner in a race to France in 1949. And during his early days of cruising round the north Irish coast, he derived lots of fun from pitting his seafaring skills against those of local fishermen in innocent but keenly fought competitions.

This chapter is presented by Mike Tinne, a lifelong friend of Wallace's whose extended family – a formidable clan of Liverpool traders, Oxford dons and oarsmen – have been holidaying or living at Culdaff in Inishowen for well over a century. While spending most of his latter years in Arizona and California, indulging his passion for tinkering with second-hand cars, Mike has always remained close to his English and Irish roots. He was a daily visitor to the Mid-Ulster hospital during Wallace's final months in spring 2011, and the old ship-mates were able to refresh each other's memories of some early adventures. In this introduction, Mike describes how Wallace got involved in a local regatta, very soon after they met, before Wallace recounts regattas at both Glengad and Culdaff.

Mike:

*O*ne day, during one of those happy postwar summers when I returned to our holiday home at the mouth of the Culdaff river, I saw a yacht sailing into the bay and anchoring. Other than fishing trawlers coming from Fleetwood in Lancashire, very few boats came into Culdaff bay. When a boat did arrive, we always ran down to the nearby quay at Bunagee, jumped into our dinghies and went alongside to welcome the visiting craft.

On this occasion, it turned out that Wallace Clark was skipper of the fine yacht and he immediately invited us on board for a wee dram. I had never met him before but we soon became good friends. A year or two later, Wallace sailed his yacht into Culdaff Bay again, where a regatta was taking place and was quickly persuaded to enter the race for craft with one mast and a jib. On the downwind leg of the race, he was surprisingly left behind by the flat-bottomed fishing boats, and he was subjected to some unkind teases, such as, "Look at you and your fancy yacht, we're beating you!" It was a different story once the boats turned round the buoy off Galavoir Point and were heading into the wind. The fishing boats were crabbing across the water, *tacking way out to sea or dangerously close to rocks inshore. I'll let Wallace tell you what happened after that, but safe to say that he had earned the fishermens' lasting respect by the day's end!*

Wallace:

During the first summer we owned *Fugitive* we took her along to the Glengad Regatta. It was the big event of the season on the Inishowen coast in the years around 1950. We had left Portrush at 0500, drawn from our pipe cots as from wells of treacle to catch the west-going tide, and came over on a broad reach with a southeast wind. Now it was a fresh southwest, coming off the cliffs in gusts and ready to blow us back. The crew for the race consisted of brother Henry, a hefty 13 stoner, with Elizabeth and Diana, both rather light-weight for working sheets and runners in a breeze, but very welcome in the roles of 'Lookout' and 'Buoy-watcher'.

Few fishermen have such an exposed anchorage as Portaleen. Several of the families now fishing from here formed, until 1936, the tiny community on Inishtrahull, nine miles away to the north where today four lighthouse keepers, one dog and about a million rabbits are the only regular inhabitants. A visiting yacht was something of a novelty and sure of a welcome.

In the brilliant sun the brown and white spritsails of the assembling fleet, weaving complicated patterns against the black and green of the cliff scenery and the sparkling sea, made an unforgettable picture. The rocks and grass banks around the pier were thickly dotted with onlookers; brightly painted motor boats filled with others dashed to and fro, while across the water came the strains of gramophone music, punctuated by the blaring notes of an ice-cream cart's horn. Close above it all, the steep slopes and rounded head of Croagh Glengad, clothed in a fascinating patchwork of tiny fields set with white cottages and brown turf stacks, formed a magnificent backcloth to the whole scene.

We were caught napping by 'The Start' when it came. Sails were brailed in and the competitors under oars formed a rough line some distance past the buoys. At 'The Gun' canvas shot up on the sprits with a smartness many a Solent racing crew might envy. We had missed the point of this manoeuvring and were 50 yards astern. How our Bermudan rig and deep keel would show up against the field we were anxiously wondering. Our rivals were all open fishing boats, 28-foot LWL to our 17-foot, carrying twin spritsails, and a baggy jib set on a temporary bowsprit, secured with its heel lashed to the mast and no bobstay. Built at Moville on the Foyle, they have a moderate beam and peculiarly fine stern. Several hundredweight of stone ballast and a powerful crew mostly clad in Sunday blue and neat cloth caps completed their racing outfit.

On the broad reach to the first buoy *Fugitive* dropped slowly back. The next leg we could just lay the mark close-hauled, and barely held our own. The big grey and blue boats tore through the water ahead of us, their bows reminiscent of destroyers. In spite of sagging sprits they held a surprisingly high wind, and made a long and short board of it. The course finished with a close reach, lacking a straight turn to windward which we hoped would have given us a chance. We could just carry our No 2 jib; getting in the sheets was hard work, and the rail right under in the gusts. With big crews sitting out the fishermen stood well up to their full canvas, while on the lee side a couple of hands seemed to keep steadily bailing. We were to windward though astern now, and could see the splash of the water being thrown up. Last year this race was sailed on a becalmed afternoon and the winner, who was actually last across the line, won, he says, because he had no bail-can; all the other boats were disqualified for using theirs as paddles!

Second time around, two boats had trouble with their sprits and gave up. We overtook one laggard on the wind, and came in a poor fourth. Tail-enders are further handicapped by the near invisibility of the buoys, black or green fishing floats with no top mark. A motorboat goes ahead and shows them to the leaders, but had usually moved on to the next one before we were near enough to be sure of the spot. We tied up to the mark-boat and brewed some tea to recuperate.

Every cruiser should race once in a while; as well as giving exhilaration undreamed of, 40 minutes of it in such a splendid breeze had shown up shortcomings in our gear which had slipped by in a season's cruising; a sheet lead better several inches further forward and some extra purchase to get in the last inch needed by the big jib in this wind, we noted.

We could race again, someone told us – there was a pleasant vagueness about the programme – this time in the 'One sail and jib' class; the same boats would compete with foremast only stepped. A better start, and we kept fairly well in the bunch, dropping back as before on the broad reach, but creeping up thrillingly inch by inch on the wind. The fishermen seemed to balance just as well and lose little speed with the single mast. Their crews' handling of the rig, an unusual one nowadays, was a constant pleasure to watch. Clever use of spars is made to bear out the loose foot of the spritsails; vangs to the head of the sprit, as often used in the Mediterranean, we did not see, but the boats lack beam for efficient use of these, and also simplicity is the keynote of the rig. Slowness in stays is their inevitable handicap, so there is no short tacking – quickest move of all is handing the sprit and brailing in all sail, as indeed it needs to be for safe sailing of undecked boats in these waters. Sails are scarcely used at all nowadays, except at perhaps three or four regattas in the summer; the motorboats carry a lug for use should the engine break down, but it is not often needed.

Our second race was enlivened by the judge's motorboat rather rashly cutting between us and the boat ahead to sustain a damaged rudder from violent contact with our bowsprit, itself unscratched. Good old *Fugitive*; Hilditch's, who built you 50 years ago, knew what they were doing. As was again proved minutes later when I disgraced myself by failing to see a big grey boat cutting across us on the starboard tack, and only came about in time to escape with a monster beam-on crash. Again no damage!

That finished our day's racing. It was a pity to miss the six-oared race, rowed in those same boats later on (time unspecified!), but anxious to save our tide, we picked up the dinghy, landed Diana and set off with a soldier's wind for home. Slowly Glengad Head sank into the sea astern, silhouetted by the evening sun. Meanwhile supper sizzled on the primus under Henry's expert care. Three hours later we slipped between well-known pier heads, ghosted to our mooring, and were soon asleep.

Saturday morning, a month later, found *Fugitive* off Bunagee where the strange sight of pink bunting fluttered bravely across the pier. Another regatta! – as we shortly discovered – was scheduled there on the following day, the first here for many years.

The wind was settled in the southwest and under these conditions Culdaff is a perfect anchorage indeed. At Portaleen, when the sky clouds over, the cliffs seem rather rapacious, glowering in their closeness, but here gentle grass slopes lead back from the pier, past whitewashed cottages and boathouse. Even the burnt-out Coastguard station, relic of stormier days, has acquired a mellow friendly look. Beyond a low rocky promontory, where terns scream defiantly, is the river mouth from which Bunagee is named, and west of it a mile of the most golden sand you ever saw. Behind this, in a wonderful variety of clear colour, lie sand hills, Culdaff House looking out from the comfortable shelter of its trees, the village roofs, and, in the background, the gaunt black cone of Slieve Snaght, highest peak in Inishowen.

The next morning heads were thick. Ashore the Guinness never runs out, nor does the whiskey, and hospitality had been lavish. We cured ourselves as best might be with a plunge over the side, and combined it with a scrub around *Fugitive's* dirty waterline. Eggs for breakfast would help too we decided. My sister Jill (who had been camping ashore) went off to the nearest farm to purchase some but, alas, the entire first dozen eggs came to grief en route back to the boat. "Well, it's jolly hard to ride a bike with one hand and stop eggs falling through the bottom of a bag with the other!" Replacements eventually reached us, but not before two more had joined their fallen comrades, this time on the stone steps of the pier where they remained a greasy snare for the unwary for the rest of the day. The survivors, however, tasted all the better for the waiting.

One by one the competitors arrived, sailing round from Portaleen, and joined the thickening crowds ashore. The wind, which had been strong in the morning, fell steadily all day, which I noted gladly, for we lacked Henry's brawn to man the sheets, and had a very light crew. Glorious periods of bright blue sky punctuated the afternoon, but there were still fierce squalls every hour or so, bringing torrential rain in their train.

Not such strangers this time, we were beckoned alongside the mark-boat for a welcome 'half un'; there was a fine stock on board for the necessary refreshment of competitors. We watched the 'Two sail and jib' class go away dead before the wind on the first leg, with a big high-peaked spritsail blowing out on either side looking like a pair of pricked-up cat's ears from astern. The 'punts' sailing race soon followed, and their departure was no small relief, for one of them with a great spread of dirty brown canvas and a wicked looking bowsprit as long as the boat, had been putting in some hard practise, turning in small circles between us where we lay at anchor and the pier, missing our topsides by successively narrower margins in his enthusiasm; eventually Jill bringing off a visitor, a VIP in fact, in the canvas dinghy, met him in unequal collision half way, and amidst a chorus of contradictory instructions yelled from the pier, scraped down his side with the gunwhale dipping under, and narrowly averted disaster.

An hour or two later, after a slow race, the big boats were back, ready for the 'One sail and jib' class. We had landed the outboard engine plus all petrol and water, and now joined them. They politely waited for us to work into position. On the run we dropped steadily astern once more, not enjoying their backward glances. Even the *Popeye*, a 25-foot motorboat, whose crew had sportingly dropped off her propeller to enter, left us ignominiously sitting. At the first buoy off Dunmore Head we lay last by 50 yards of a well strung-out fleet of eight. Thirty seconds later – I still wonder how it happened – having grazed past the buoy and come close-hauled for the long windward leg, we found ourselves ahead of all but one boat. The fishermen just seemed to stop as they came on the wind in the light airs, and were rapidly swept to leeward by the tide. A thrilling transformation for us, which we spared no effort to make good, for a squall might alter the picture at any moment. A few minutes sufficed to catch the leader – it was light grey, the boat we had hit at Glengad – and after that we were further aided by finding a better breeze inshore than the others, still struggling with the tide in the middle of the bay. So across the line to the sound of the gun, alongside the mark-boat for the 'other half', and a £6 prize; it was a great moment, and a fine end to the season.

CHAPTER 4
First Time to Brittany
Neophyte Navigators, 1952

Bruce:

As Wallace later recalled, his trip to Brittany, at 25, marked his first taste of the 'thrill of being a real skipper' on a boat that was out of sight of land and heading for a foreign shore. Although Wallace was no modern linguist, he could overcome most barriers. On arrival at Brest he made a life-long friend: a lad in his late teens who helped Caru to find a mooring and shared Wallace's passions for boats and for the social opportunities seafaring can bring. Bernard Felix spoke movingly at a luncheon in memory of Wallace in January 2012, hosted by the Irish and Royal Cruising Clubs, about a yachting and social relationship over six decades.

Bernard writes:

As Wallace explains in this account of his first trip to Brittany, we met when he sailed into Brest and I jumped on board Caru. I was instantly impressed not only by Wallace's seamanship but by his capacity to communicate with people in all circumstances. His spontaneous friendships embraced many of my compatriots, humble and grand. Let me supplement Wallace's memories with a few of my own.

After we left Brest, we took in the scenery of that magnificent sound and landed to the south at Landévennec, famous for its monastery where Wallace's son Bruce made a pilgrimage in 2010; and also for the 'graveyard' of naval vessels near the mouth of the river Aulne. The village is picturesque and we dined in a modest café-bar. After the meal we settled in the snug and chatted to two gendarmes. After toasts to eternal friendship, our companions would have faced embarrassment if their sobriety had been tested. So instead of riding back to the station, they returned on foot, pushing their bicycles unsteadily. In the heat of the conversation, Wallace had spoken of his life in the services, and he asked one of our new friends to procure a second-hand gendarme's uniform. Our companion agreed. Wallace was a man of his word and he expected the same of others. So the next morning we went to the premises where the gendarmes lived and worked. It was closed, so Wallace knocked and the wife of one of our police friends opened a small window and crossly demanded to know what the matter was. Wallace said we had come to get the promised uniform from our police friend, let's call him Loic. We heard a tetchy conversation between *the couple until Loic appeared with the kit. Wallace put the uniform on – to general hilarity because it was too small. What if we met some more real gendarmes? In that remote place it seemed unlikely.*

We left Landévennec late in the day because we needed a fresh tide to reach the lock of Port-Launay and Châteaulin beyond. The Aulne is a beautiful piece of water. Sadly Caru got stuck before reaching the lock. It was pointless to jump ship to the muddy banks. With the boat immobilised we decided to enjoy a good dinner. I flambéed an omelette in rum, on deck for safety's sake. After soothing our spirits with some beverages, we fell into a deep sleep – so deep that when we awoke, the tide was again falling and Caru was again sinking. We arrived at Châteaulin a day late. Some time afterwards, we found ourselves in Bénodet and turned into the Odet which is the most beautiful river in France. At every bend, we would come across splendid estates. One morning at breakfast-time, we found ourselves in front of a pleasant little chateau. The proprietors came down to meet us on the lawn which swept down to the river-bank, and invited us to share their breakfast. The châtelain was an ambassador and we drank to international friendship. But another early-morning encounter had a less happy outcome. Exploring a canal bank, we came across a little winery where we greeted the proprietor and were invited to join him for brunch. He gave us a glass demijohn containing 25 litres of wine. After sampling his produce, we took our leave. But as we were manhandling the demijohn on board Caru, it smashed and the deck was covered in a deep shade of red, which I can still see. Now let Wallace take up the story.

Wallace:

I had just bought *Caru*, a curvaceous, five-ton sloop designed and built by McGruer on the Clyde. Every mahogany plank of her hull had been hand-picked and each joint filled with a matching spine. Her 'bright work', as sailors call varnish, gleamed in a faultless sheen as befitted a prize winner at the Glasgow Exhibition in 1938. Measuring 27-feet overall with an eight-foot beam and short bowsprit, her 20-foot waterline gave a speed of six knots under sail. The seven HP Baby Austin petrol engine produced four knots under power. That meant we should manage an average of 100 nautical miles in a 24-hour day.

A weekend passage was needed to get *Caru* 200 miles south to Wexford. For this leg, it was a pleasure to have on board Jan Eccles, a horticulturalist who had spent a lifetime sailing out of Milk Harbour in Donegal Bay. Mervyn Henry, a Coleraine racing yachtsman, completed the crew.

In glorious weather, we slipped our moorings at 2000 hours on Wednesday, 10 May. There was no wind, but the donk plus an east-going spring tide carried us 30 miles round magnificent Fair Head, just beyond Ballycastle, by midnight. Then the weather thickened up. At 0400 hours, as dawn should have been breaking, visibility was less than 100 yards in a white mist. It was time to steer west to sight the Antrim coast and find out how far we had travelled. This stretch is blessedly clear of outlying rocks and a lead line sounding indicated land half a mile off. The first indication that we were really getting warm came from Jan on lookout in the bow. "I hear a thrush singing quite close," she called. Still nothing could be seen, but we altered course to the southeast and crept on. Sure enough, two minutes later there was the thrush on top of a tree and Ballygally Hotel in the mist behind it. So remember to put your birdwatchers on fog lookout!

Through intermittent patches of fog, we reached Wexford harbour 30 hours later. There was excellent anchorage below the bridge in the harbour and in those days there were no harbour dues. We knew *Caru* was safe there for as long as we liked to leave her. We said goodbye to Jan and welcomed on board, for the French leg, Alan Smiles, a red faced, jolly member of the Royal North of Ireland Yacht Club, who had sailed round the west of Ireland with me the year before.

We had enough juice for 200 miles under engine alone, 300 if assisted even by a Force 2 wind. Enough to bring us there and back. We had eight gallons of water, sufficient for eight days with economies such as washing up and cooking in salt water. Porridge tastes better with one third salt water. "You can live for 40 days without food, but only six without water, Wally," Alan remarked, as we handed items into the main hatch. "But we gotta have enough whiskey. Sailing's a tough game, Wally, and you've always got to look for the compensations!"

Outside the harbour we found a head on, southwesterly, Force 4 wind in which we could just lay the course for the Tuskar – the graceful white lighthouse that lies ten miles east of Carnsore Point, denoting the southeasterly extreme of Ireland. Clear of the land there was a three-foot sea; *Caru* took it in her stride. She loved going to windward. At 1400 hours we handed the No 1 jib and set the big Genoa. Later the wind freshened and backed until the rail was awash, and we were making four knots on course for Land's End. The motion below was lively and as these conditions persisted for the next 24 hours, we began to feel the strain. We were still a day or two short of acquiring our sea legs. "The Yanks say a five tonner isn't a yacht, Wally, just an instrument for inflicting torture," was Alan's comment. But he was happy… as he always was at sea. We worked two-hour solo watches, so in theory you had four hours off in between spells at the tiller. But there were usually jobs below. Alan did all the cooking at sea, sharing it in harbour with Mervyn, while navigation and engine care was mainly my pigeon.

Mervyn regaled us with the tale of how one dark night during the war, watchers from the shore saw the Tuskar had failed to light. It emerged that the keepers were 'tapping the Admiral': a barrel of spirits from a war-time sinking had come ashore and been enjoyed. The phrase came from the time when Nelson's body had been put in a cask of rum for preservation. Sailors with strong stomachs drilled a hole and glugged away.

The steering compass was an ex RAF luminous five-inch grid type. With a pair of parallel lines on top which could be swivelled to line up with the needle on the required course, it was almost fool-proof. Instead of a deviation card to correct for possible errors from iron objects (tools for instance) near the compass, I checked the ship's head by standing on deck, clear of any magnetic anomalies, with a hand bearing compass, also ex RAF – a well tried system which never failed. For a check on position we used a radio beacon known as Consol which emits a series of dots and dashes from stations at Bushmills in Ireland and Plonéis in France. Counting them gave a position line accurate to within a mile.

At lunch-time on Sunday we sighted Hartland Point in Cornwall five miles off, and behind it a pleasantly familiar peak. We had been forced well east of Land's End and now had to make 38 miles in a southwesterly direction in a series of five-mile tacks. "Bother this for a game of sailors," said Alan. At 1730 hours we lost the land again amid fog horns all around us. A few hours later, visibility had improved and the moon was so bright that I called to Alan to pass up sunglasses as I searched for the Seven Stones Lightship. By 0655 hours we were well 'Round the Land' abreast the isolated Wolf Rock. A flat calm with a few puffy clouds in a blue sky marked the start of a perfect day.

At 1800 we were 55 miles off the Four Tower at the north end of the Ouessant inshore channel. That was fine and dandy, but our arrival there would be just at the beginning of the north going tide, so it seemed best to bear off for L'Abervrach, just east of the entrance. At midnight another excitement, as Mervyn called, "Land Ho!" on sighting the loom of Creach Light on Ouessant 30 miles off. Tremendous claps of thunder roared over us with forked lightning crackling near the masthead. I shorted its circuit in the approved fashion by attaching a length of wire to the rigging to hang in the water over the side. Even as I made it sparks ran down past me, but nothing happened to my gloved fists. As we stared in awe, the low black Brittany coast was illuminated by flashes for quite long periods, extending five miles in either direction. Then rain came in torrents.

In half an hour the greatest heavenly show I had witnessed was over. In the absence of wind it took full revs on the motor to drive us to the Baie de Lampaul on the southwest end of the island. There the north-going stream was just getting into its stride and running strongly past the entrance. The chart showed this narrowed by reefs on either side, with a high rocky island in the middle. With no room to tack, we motored in with the mainsail flapping madly, keeping right on the leading marks which were very clear. At the narrowest part the wind gusted up, and I saw a two-foot seam near the head of the sail start to split. The crew got it down in a hurry. At 0730 we anchored off the inner harbour. Breakfast tea was well spiked with whiskey before we turned in for three hours. Then the excitement of a first run ashore in a strange country.

"Alors," said a girl expectantly from behind a bar. She had watched us row ashore and wanted to hear our story. "Formidable…" I stammered. Then Alan put in: "Nous venons de l'Irlande." There was disbelief. Yachts from England on this coast were rare, and few called at Ouessant. Yachts from Ireland were virtually unknown. Handshakes followed, free drinks, offers of *dejeuner* and a tour of the village. Back on board, we began to snug down for a rough passage to Brest as the breeze gusted fiercely. But inside an hour, as the tide turned south, the day changed wonderfully. In hot sunshine we bent on the new cotton mainsail for a final stretch. It was the sort of weather we had come for.

Six hours later we entered the narrow rocky entrance to the ten-mile long Rade de Brest. The waterfront side of the city of Brest was a heap of white rubble. The British had been bombing the German submarines in the area throughout World War II and never hit the harbour or city once. The Americans arrived at the end of the war and flattened the city. Another relic of war consisted of two large pillars built up from the bottom of Brest's harbour where the *Bismarck* would have been tied up, had the Royal Navy not hunted her down and sunk her.

We had been told to berth in the Port de Commerce, but we were waved away and wondered where to try. Then a French teenager, walking with his parents, offered to pilot us round to the yacht moorings at the eastern end of the harbour. He leapt aboard and introduced himself as Bernard Felix. The sunken wrecks made us glad of Bernard's help and he readily accepted an invitation to join us for an exploration of the Rade de Brest the following day.

Once anchored Bernard and Mervyn went ashore in our canvas dinghy and sent a motor boat back to collect myself and Alan. We asked the boatman on board for a glass of 'Irish wine' and when he got back on board his own boat again nothing would start the engine. After cursing he threw the starting handle overboard with a truly Gallic gesture, and proceeded to scull the heavy boat, some 30-feet long, back to the shore against quite a stiff breeze. Bretons are born seamen.

The next morning Bernard proved an excellent pilot. We spent two days exploring the Rade de Brest, getting to know the area. Thus began our long friendship. Bernard was the only son of Breton parents who ran a chain of department stores under the title Aux Dames de France. Their Brest one, flattened in the bombing, was trading in wooden hutments erected on the rubble, with the tricolour flying above Tremazan.

(Bernard sailed with us in Scotland the following year. In 1957, he hitched a lift in a fishing boat to Ireland, to be an extra best man at my wedding. The fishing boat was due to land on the southwestern corner of Ireland, but Bernard got hold of the deviation card and compass and changed the bearings so they would land near Wexford. This would shorten the next leg of his trip up to our wedding in County Down. Something went wrong with Bernard's calculations and the boat arrived in Limerick. He still got to the wedding on time. Nine years later, my wife, June, and I would visit Tremazan and the Felix family with our sons, Bruce and Miles. Aged seven, Bruce learned to swim and practised French and Breton. Not many years later, June and I would visit Madame Felix at their home near Toulon where we borrowed Bernard's boat, *Skreo*, and sailed to the Isles de Levant.)

We left Brest on 3 July with a strong ebb tide which squirted us west like a pip out of an orange. Then we bore away past Camaret for the Toulinguet Passage, which saves going right out to La Parquette tower which lies at the end of a chain of sunken rocks, seven miles long. We were travelling so fast on the favourable tide that it was vital to be 'on the ball' with pilotage.

French buoys are tall and easy to pick up at a distance, but I did not master the system of marks which indicate the direction of the danger.

Just south of the Toulinguet and from there to Les Tas de Pois is some of the finest rocky coastal scenery we saw, but, while being an entrancing cruising ground, the scenery in Brittany does not compare with the Irish or west of Scotland coasts.

The breeze dropped again as we approached the Raz de Sein and, arriving as we did, exactly on slack water neaps, there was not a ripple to indicate that there is a race there at all. Just south of it a fisherman in a small motorboat drew alongside to offer us two spider crabs which almost filled the cockpit. We thanked him with a mug of Irish whiskey which he swallowed in two gulps.

At 0930 the next morning we motored up into the Audierne River in a northerly, Force 6 squall, amid blinding rain. A Frenchman waved from the quay, and when we drew alongside, he came on board saying he was the pilot. He directed us, mostly in Breton, to an anchorage below the bridge where there is a hole under the north and south arches. He put us, however, on a bank well below the north hole. We realised he was an alcoholic, so set him ashore and laid out the kedge to warp back into the hole. We got the bower and started to move, but had not realised the strength of the tide where it is constricted by the bridge. The kedge dragged, the wind which had been helping to hold us against the tide suddenly dropped, and we were carried straight under the bridge. We started the engine instantly, but almost too late and the mast seemed doomed. We struck the north pier hard then scraped clear only to see the port spreader go with a splintering crack. But by this time the engine was going well which helped to slowly work the boat's head round and punch her out. The top six inches were cracked off the transom by the backstay, having caught under an arch – that and the spreader were all the harm. Inside an hour we had a French shipwright on board. He finished work at 2200 and cheerfully started again at 0600 the following morning in the pouring rain, which continued all day. With his skilled help we were ready for sea in 24 hours.

By 1300 on Sunday, 6 July, we were running inside Belle Ile then turned in through the Teignouse Channel. Passing many French yachts, big and small, we ghosted across Quiberon Bay to La Trinité, a great French yachting centre on the Crach River where we spent the night. The next day, we were underway again by late morning and after two hours we reached the

Gulf of Morbihan, a French Strangford Lough, far the most beautiful place we visited. The flood tide was running at six knots at the entrance, and the wind fell very light just at the focal point of the tides, as it so often seems to. Past here, it breezed up again and we had a fine sail on the bluest of water among lovely islets with sandy beaches and low rocky points, all clad in dark pine and cypress. On one islet we met Nicole and Claude Tual, daughters of an admiral. They were to remain life-long friends.

We could have happily stayed a week, cruising at leisure, but we had to press north again. Out through the Teignouse Channel, we next sailed for the Ile de Groix, 20 miles away. En route, we spent the night at Port Tudy – the home of the last few sailing tunnymen. These were traditional fisher boats geared for catching tunny (tuna), and we were lucky to pass quite close to one running very fast with his great red reaching jib boomed out as a spinnaker, and long rods lowered down on either beam with about ten baited lines attached to each one. Port Tudy was fascinating, and although we could not find a suitable berth in the small harbour, we decided that it was worth the discomfort of grounding *Caru* for a couple of hours overnight to prolong our visit. I am glad we did, for that same evening a French fisherman came on board with a bag of sardines and cooked them on our stove, singing the while. The Belon River was only a short sail the next morning, and we passed many small open luggers with patched, multi-coloured sails, fishing in the sunshine. The Belon port was our favourite port of all. Peaceful and unspoilt, we were told we were the first yacht there this year.

On arrival at Concarneau harbour we found a comfortable berth clear of the great bunch of deeper draft boats moored in the middle of the harbour. It was market day and we spent the morning shopping and wandering. Too hot for comfort ashore, we were happy to leave Concarneau at lunchtime. A pleasant sailing breeze greeted us as we tacked for our next port of call. Bénodet, on a bend of the lovely tree-clad River Odet is a justly popular yachting centre. We visited the famous Henriot China Foundry where, for six pounds, I purchased the life-size head and shoulders of a stern Breton fisherman in traditional beret. He still adorns our kitchen.

We departed Bénodet at 2300 and, once outside, found the array of white, red and green flashing lights a little bewildering. The Anse, the area that we were now entering, is notorious for its rocks, and as we headed west there were at least nine lighthouses in sight but nary a lit buoy to mark the outside of the reefs that extended south from the coast, and northeast from the Ile aux Moutons. Many of these once lit buoys were destroyed by the Germans, and our course lay in the narrow gap between them. The hand bearing compass was in constant use over the next few hours. At 0200 I got a fright. We were well heeled, and having just had a look round the horizon, I was concentrating on watching the leach of the Genoa on the lee side, when over the angle of the coach roof, high out of the water, and about 20 feet away, I glimpsed a solid looking object on top of a stick, coming straight at us. As I leapt for the weather side, I was quite convinced it was the mast of an unlit fishing boat about to cut us in half, but was just in time to see nothing more deadly than a crab pot buoy sliding passed with a tall withy (cane) and tattered flag on top of it.

At 0930 the next morning we anchored off the beach at Audierne and had a dash ashore for coffee and croissants. Off again at 1100 in bright sunlight and a light wind, we were late getting to the Raz de Sein. It was about an hour after slack water, and as we approached one solid line of white breakers met the eye from La Veille tower to Tevennec. We were soon carried into the maelstrom, and almost as quickly out of it, decks hardly splashed. There was no anger in it, for the wind was not above a Force 2, but I can still see those curling white crests close alongside, some feet above our heads as we crouched low in *Caru's* cockpit, beautiful as ballet dancers in the bright sunlight, and yet a reminder of what the Raz would be like in slightly less favourable conditions. From here, a 20-mile reach eastwards, along the rocky shore, took us to Douarnenez, a lively town. We soon found what we needed in the town's harbour, Port de Rosmur, before the approaching homeward journey – a food store run by the stout Robert Jacques, who was proud of his war-time service in England. After the order was complete he stood us a rum, then a large port. We purchased perishables and *vin ordinaire*, for our stock of tins had lasted well. Bread was a problem. French loaves are brick hard after 24 hours. You could buy buns made of fine flour, something like our loaves, but dearer. We bought some anyway and eked them out with lifeboat biscuits. We left the stores on board and came back for a glass of wine at the Loups du Mer café, where the owner showed us a postcard of Berehaven from her husband whose trawler was fishing off the Kerry coast. As if France knew of our departure and was giving us a last fling, we were invited to a *Grand Bal* in the village hall, where we stole some dances with the *Reine de la Fête* – Festival Queen.

After 12 hours at sea the following day, with slow progress in light winds through a jumbled swell to begin with, followed by no wind at all, a temporarily dead engine, then wind again, it occurred to us that to keep our schedule we would have to motor continuously. Having traced and fixed a faulty ignition the night before, at 0600 we restarted the engine. At 0800 the stern gland began to sound as if a woodpecker was hard at it from the outside. This seemed unlikely; of more importance was a steady trickle of water coming from behind the inner flange. We were about eight miles from St Margarets so we decided to head there, tie alongside the pier and as the tide dropped, dry out the boat in order to detect the problem.

We were afloat again that night and set out for New Grimsby Sound full of renewed confidence. It was narrow, and parts of it dry, but the tide was still flooding and we felt like having a go. Hugh Town Pier Light and the loom of St Mary's lighthouse in transit put us onto the beacon at the end of the sound, but once past the shelter of the pier it was very difficult to hold onto this line with a fresh beam wind and cross tide. The night was dark, and half way across the bay we decided to turn back and anchor until daylight. Once clear of a rip tide off the Scillies at dawn the following day, we found an even beam sea and low swell with a splendid breeze and really started to travel. The blood was up, and we started a competition as to who could get the most miles on the log for his watch.

At 0600 the following day, heading straight for Carnsore Point, Mervyn sighted land in the form of Forth Mountain, and by the next afternoon we had arrived at the south end of Dundrum Bay. After that, our first stop-off after days at sea was Strangford village and the point of departure for Mervyn. We'd had a cracking passage home.

John White, a Dublin cousin, adds:

Wallace made many voyages to Brittany, and invariably the first port of call was Ouessant Island. On one trip, our landfall on Ouessant was a quiet harbour with no sign of life. Refreshment was available only on the other side of the island. We saw some bikes lying against a wall with no obvious owner, so the four of us hopped on them and headed for the hostelries. As we wobbled back, we were stopped by the bikes' irate owner. All Wallace said was: "Nous sommes irlandais!" That calmed things down. We paid some francs and all was well.

CHAPTER 5
A Viking Returns to Norway
From Ireland to the Fjords of Norway and back, 1953

Bruce:

By 1953, Wallace was already an accomplished deep-water yachtsman, but ploughing across the North Sea to the fjords of Scandinavia in a small boat was still a courageous and (at the time) unusual undertaking. His arrival was written up enthusiastically in the Norwegian press. Perhaps Wallace's Viking qualities drew some flicker of recognition in his hosts. This chapter is introduced by Garry Villiers-Stuart. Garry and above all his father Mike were lifelong friends of Wallace with a common love for sturdy old wooden boats. Wallace, Mike and Garry made a later voyage to Norway, and as of 2012 Garry is probably the only person alive who can describe what it was like to sail with Wallace across the North Sea.

Garry:

I don't know how my Dad and Wallace first met up, maybe during World War II or just after, but it was not long before a firm friendship developed between them. There was the Northern Irish connection, there was their respective links with family firms, but they were especially connected through their passion for all things to do with sea and boats. As I grew up Wallace became as synonymous with his boat **Wild Goose** as my Dad was with his beloved **Winny**. The age discrepancy between them was such that in those early years, while my father was heavy with children and consequent family responsibilities, Wallace was still fancy free. So it must have been sweet windows of opportunity when Wallace would invite my Dad to join him in this or that sailing adventure. Reading the log of Wallace's Norwegian voyage reminded me of the time when Dad, having spent a small fortune refitting **Winny**, invited Wallace to be part of **Winny**'s first big post refit sailing adventure; to Norway and back. Us children were now teenagers, but Dad needed an experienced crew member to compliment the youngsters. Wallace was up for it. Like the voyage fifteen years earlier, we sailed from Belfast Lough through the Caledonian Canal to Inverness in order to make the North Sea passage to Norway. Similarly we made for Utsira Island. RDF direction finders were still the highest tech way of electronic navigation… dots to be counted, direction to be recorded.

A boat is a great way of getting to know people. So this was the time that I first grew to really appreciate the many good qualities that Wallace brought to life. There was his big heartedness, his kindness, his nautical skills and his treasure house of stories which he told with a nod to the ways of delivery by the ancient Irish seanachaís (story tellers). We listened to many good tales as we made that unhurried passage across that North Sea. The Norway we visited was much the same as the one described in the first log. The Norwegians still held the English and Irish in high regard. They were very friendly, Bergen was still a delightful town built mainly out of wood. The Norwegians loved the dram but found whiskey hard to come by, so we were able to do great trade swopping duty-free whiskey or gin for fresh sea trout or salmon. For Wallace, our voyage (in the 60s) must have bought back many memories of his early 50s voyage.

Happily for us Wallace remained a great family friend right down to his dying day. That very good soul is no longer with us... but for those of us who held Wallace in high regard, reading his log is a wonderful way to bring him back into mind.

Wallace:

From the Met Office statistics in the Norway Coast Pilot Part II, and the North Sea Pilot, Parts II and III, July appeared to be the best month to go. There would be an 8-1 chance of a fair wind passage over and an even chance of a fair one back in the month of July. June would be marginally better but not as warm, and the average wind strength and frequency of gales about the same for either month. Gales blow on average two or three days per month, so that given two four-day crossings, the chances of meeting one in the open are evens. One would have to be prepared for plenty of rain on the Norwegian Coast – Bergen outdoes Manchester as the rainy city, having an annual rainfall of around 76 inches in which its inhabitants take an inverted pride. July it was then, and in preparation for the cruise, along with a ten-day supply of food and the usual complicated assembly of gear, tools, spares, water and fuel, I fitted a homemade folding canvas spray hood onto *Caru* to cover the forward half of the cockpit. Another important accessory would be her Austin Seven engine as auxiliary power. *Caru* in fresh, fair winds can average six knots and a cruising speed under engine with sails just drawing enough to keep them quiet of four knots. With no sail up (which rarely occurs) speed is under three and a half knots and petrol consumption about 40 per cent more.

The crew for the trip consisted of Robin Snead-Cox, a retired Welsh Guards Colonel, Gerry Gailey, a Mackies trained engineer, and my skipper-self. We slipped from Portrush harbour, County Antrim, under engine, on the last Wednesday of June at 1900 hours. Visibility was poor, the sea almost flat calm, with only the faintest of cat's paws ruffling the surface. At 0200 we made Scotch landfall on Cath Sgeir Buoy, west of Gigha. Onwards we motored up to the Sound of Jura, the sails just drawing at times, and as dawn brought no sign of wind, pressed on under power passing through the Dorus Mor at 1040, and the Fladan Light by 1240.

At 1400 hours, just south of Duart Narrows, we tried the spinnaker for a while but soon had to give it up – the wind was too light. The lack of wind was annoying, but more-so the poor visibility, preventing us from enjoying the scenery. The rest of the day passed uneventfully, but we had to keep motoring to enable us to get through the Caledonian Canal before Sunday. At 2100 we anchored just north of Corran Narrows, Loch Linnhe. Ashore, we bought some petrol and had dinner at the nearby hotel. Seven miles to go to the mouth of the Canal.

A 0400 'Wakey, Wakey' brought yet more fog, a thick haze, with a maximum visibility of 50 yards. The anchor buoy rope caught round the prop when getting underway, but fortunately not badly, and a few minutes of anxious fidgeting cleared it. We smelled our way up the north shore which was fairly clean, visibility slowly improving, and entered the sea loch at Corpach at 0700. A large notice with 'Caledonian Canal' greeted us. This was, as Robin remarked, reassuring.

By 0940 we had reached the top of Neptune's Staircase – the Benavie Locks – with 11 behind us in two and three quarter hours. The day steadily improved. By the time we entered Loch Lochy it was off shirts and hands to sunbathe with the lovely green, pine-clad shores of the loch-side scenery looking at their best, and perfectly mirrored in the bright blue water. Five hours later and we were through Laggan Loch at the head of Loch Lochy, the ascent completed – 15 locks in all. And then we ran aground. It was in one of the reaches about half a mile short of Kitra Loch. This really seemed like 'one below the belt'. The mud must have been real glue. After an hour of tugging and warping, we had not moved an inch though we were still floating on our normal waterline and not apparently hard on. It was beginning to look like we were about to become a permanent addition to the landscape when the Keeper from the next lock appeared on his bike, wondering what had happened to us and rather impatient as he wanted to get us through and return home for his tea. Having taken in the situation, he peddled back and rang up his chum at the last lock who opened the gates and let the waters flow. In about 40 minutes the level had risen two inches and we were off! On entering Loch Ness later that evening we found only a ghost of a wind from dead ahead so carried on motoring, anchoring eventually in Foyer's Bay, close to the river mouth where great rafts of foam had gathered, comprising rain-whipped spate from the many burns leading into the river.

The 27 of June dawned dull but dry. By the time we reached Muirtown Basin, with Inverness 11 miles away, it was 1200 and the sun was shining. As soon as we arrived at Muirtown we were met by a courteous Custom's Officer, and also Mr Frazer, a helpful and experienced Ship Chandler, to both of whom I had written ahead. Mr Frazer took down our order, made some useful suggestions in the process, and delivered it by van a couple of hours later. By 1600 hours we were out of the sea lock and into the Moray Firth. Once out of the narrows, with Fort George abeam at 1800, only the North Sea lay between us and Norway, 330 miles to the east. We had ten days food and water stowed below. The courses open to us were between 057 degrees True for Bergen and 078 degrees True for Stavanger. Utsira Island, which lies about seven miles off shore between these bearings, is the best landfall, as other parts of the coast are difficult to identify, and some have sunken reefs off lying three or four miles. The glass was high and steady, conditions seemed settled; it was an ideal start.

We tacked off Nairn at 2015, the wind now a Force 3-4, northeasterly, and a celebratory dinner 'a la Prestige' – the pressure cooker – ensued of smoked cod, new potatoes and cauliflower with white sauce. To combat public enemy No 1 – sea sickness – we left off fries for the passage, also red meat, and I regret to say, alcohol. But it was well worth it!

During the night the wind failed us and as time was precious, the engine was switched on to push us along at four knots. The whole of the next day passed uneventfully. We saw several steam trawlers, some with their gear down, and hoped there might be a chance of some fresh fish, but none came close. The wind continued to defy us. All we got were maddening little puffs from right ahead which would only last about 15 minutes.

The following day was no better. The forecast was 'winds variable, mainly northerly and light.' Conditions remained exactly the same; still warm and overcast, with not a glimpse of sun. In the afternoon I shifted the Beme Loop onto the coach roof and got quite good bearings of Kinnaird Head, and May Island Radio Direction Finder, which agreed with our Dead

Reckoning (DR) – 140 miles to go, 48 hours out and 180 miles behind us. We were now getting the Stavanger Consol quite clearly.

Another peaceful night; still not a breath except for those little puffs from dead ahead. We were becoming so used to the windless expanse that it was difficult to imagine it in any other mood. We had fuel for about 270 miles and used nearly all of it as the crossing was so calm; indeed the faithful Austin ran for about 50 hours with only a few brief stops.

'Tuesday, 30 June, 0600. Stopped engine, set Genoa'. At last! The first free breeze for two and a half days! The wind continually strengthened over the day from the northeast giving us a close-haul. The tanker, *British Rover*, passed us about 1930 and gave us a friendly hoot on her siren, duly acknowledged by dipping our red duster. By then we were sailing very fast on a close reach. *Caru* was jumping about and it was difficult for us to keep secure in the cockpit without recourse to strapping ourselves in by any means available. At about 2300 we passed close by two large modern trawlers slowly working round in circles, also pitching and rolling. A nasty, steep sea, about eight-feet high, had developed. Three hours later the Genoa ripped and a rapid change was made to the No 1 jib.

By 0800 the next day Norway was in sight in the shape of Utsira Island. Landfall at last after four nights at sea! We sailed in through the outlying skerries with a fresh, northerly breeze and a clear blue sky. The Skaergaard, an almost unbroken barrier of islets lying a mile or two off shore and running for hundreds of miles along Norway's coast, gives unlimited sheltered water for coastwise traffic as well as yachtsmen, with tens of thousands of fabulous anchorages, and forms one of the finest cruising grounds in the world. The population seemed friendly to British visitors, perhaps even more so to Irish. This led to one humorous incident. We were approaching Godosund when an elderly man in a small motorboat shouted to us in rather broken English, "Are you from England?" By the time we had called back, "No – Ireland," our boats were far apart, but he stood up in the stern and with a great smile bellowed after us a hearty, "Begorra!" ("By God!").

The first fjord we sailed into was Bommelfjord. We were struck by the large number of coasters plying up and down it, in contrast to the lack of seaborne traffic on the Scottish coast. At 1400 the anchor touched bottom in the delightful haven of Langevåg. Our first close look at Norway was pleasurable indeed: gaily painted wooden houses, some built right on the shore with gables overhanging the water, and many small double-ended skiffs pulled up on the beach. In the fields women were spreading hay, snatches of their gossip and laughter carrying over the water to us.

Inviting as the countryside looked, a meal and a sound sleep came first. In the evening we sailed on to the busy harbour of Leirvik, the largest town in the fjord. The next day, 2 July, was spent shopping. Wherever we went people were extremely helpful, and we had no difficulty in making ourselves understood as most Norwegians speak English quite well. After lunch ashore we sailed on up the fjord in perfect weather. Our anchorage for the night was Husevåg – a landlocked bay with trees reaching right down to the water's edge. We left this delectable spot mid-morning and pushed on to Rosendal by way of Stord Sund which was deep and narrow, flanked on one side by gentle slopes at the mountain foot, while on the other was a wall of sheer rock 200-feet high. After lunch at Rosendal we had an enjoyable sail to Hardanger Fjord in which was the most magnificent scenery of the entire cruise. Mountains tumbled straight into the fjord and here and there streams spilled over the cliff tops to bounce hundreds of feet down the pine-covered slopes.

As Sundal is the main village in the fjord, and starting point for trips to the glacier, we brought up for the night. We anchored in nine fathoms and ran a warp ashore to a convenient bollard, marked in typical Norwegian style by a bull's-eye painted on a rock. We went ashore early the next morning and were met by Enar, the guide with whom we had arranged to visit the glacier. At intervals, heavy single strand wires stretched from the valley floor right up the sides of the mountains used, we learned later, for transporting hay and firewood from the less accessible parts of the valley. After half an hour of climbing, a lake suddenly appeared which we crossed by boat. We then scrambled up an old track to where the glacier had deposited thousands of tons of rubble. Another 30 minutes strenuous climbing brought us to the ice. From that height, the view down the valley and across the fjord was superb – well worth the effort of the ascent.

When we left Sundal the following morning about half the population turned out to wave goodbye. The weather had returned to its former brilliance and we had a glorious sail to Norheimsund. Two more windless days were spent in the fjord and we got as far as Ulvik, about 90 miles from the sea. We enjoyed meals on shore in the spotlessly clean tourist hotels at very reasonable cost – maybe just a little more expensive than England. We discovered quickly that no spirits were on sale anywhere except in the big towns! Light beer was by far the main alcoholic beverage found ashore, so it is essential to bring your own supplies.

Navigation in the fjords was easy, the water being very deep, and the few dangers being well marked by perches and small lighthouses. We saw these working for the first time at the end of our first week. The day coincided with the opening of the new season, since no navigation lights in this part of Norway are shown from 28 May to 10 July. The little lighthouses are painted all white, are mostly hexagonal with pointed roofs, and look exactly like pigeon cots. We continued to sail right up the Hardanger against the wind, which headed us at every corner. On return, it had changed direction and we had to put up with it again. On our last day in the fjord the heavens really opened and we had our wettest day in Norway.

To get out of the fjord we passed through the narrow Lok Sund. The Sound was only 50 yards wide in places with rocky sides rising dramatically several hundred feet and looked rather sombre in the rain. The Bergen yachtsmen told us of its fierce tides with some awe, but the Admiralty pilot said three knots maximum, and we noticed none at all! Perhaps we passed through at slack water. Once through it there was a complete change of scenery, back to the low rounded hills and rocky skerries of the coast. We headed west for tree-covered Godo Island where there was a popular tourist hotel, a large red and white wooden building among the pines, with water washing its very walls. Anchored nearby we recognised *Loki*, an American ocean racer, whom we had read about in a newspaper a week earlier as having arrived at Bergen from New York. Her skipper, Dr Giff Pinchot, waved us to come alongside, and there ensued one of the merriest evenings in the company of one of the nicest crews of any nationality I have ever come across.

The next morning we all breakfasted ashore and then bade farewell to *Loki* and went our various ways: they were heading south for Cowes and the Fastnet race before shipping home, we were heading to the first big city of our trip, the ancient capital of Norway – Bergen. The Commodore of the Bergen Yacht Club had joined *Loki* for two days to pilot them through the narrow channels off the main track, and on his recommendation we followed part of the same route, which was much more fun than the big ship channel. We did it all under sail too, inspired by the crew of *Loki* – real sailors with no engine – and had the fun of picking leaves off the trees in places as we glided past. We enjoyed looking into Lonningshavn on the way past – a sketch of it by CG Lynam who visited in 1911 and recorded it in his 'Blue Dragon's Log', having particularly caught my fancy. There were a few more houses and boats at Lonningshavn now, but the inner part which he sketched was almost unchanged; an oval pool about 150-yards long which you enter by shooting through a 30-foot wide, rock-bordered entrance.

We met with an increasing amount of steamer, fishing and pleasure boat traffic up and down the main channel which we now entered. The breeze died away in the evening, and the last three miles to Bergen took almost as many hours with the spinnaker drawing badly, upset every now and then by the wash of passing traffic. We found Bergen to be a most beautiful city – gleaming white buildings, set off by the many trees showing dark green among them, lying on a low tongue of land surrounded by green hills on whose steep faces pretty dwelling houses clung in chains and clusters wherever they could. It was not large – just less than a quarter of a million in population – but very conscious of its heritage as the ancient capital.

The next day and a half passed very pleasantly about the city. A Mr Carl Gjesthal was most kind, showing us round and offering helpful suggestions with our shopping. Good ship chandlers abound; 'Gjertsens' being the pride of them all. There we bought some fine woollen seamen's jerseys at an amazingly low price. We made a number of friends, got the Genoa repaired and an electrician came back to the anchorage with us to check *Caru's* engine.

Carl Gjesthal was not only a guide during our stay, but, also, being a journalist by profession, did us proud on the front page of the 'Morgenavisen', Bergen's morning paper, the next day. The heading of the article was: "Norway and the Folgefonn Gacier made more of a hit with the shamrock of *Caru* than a 'collision' with the Loch Ness Monster." The title was, of course, referring to our going aground near Loch Ness – the assumed culprit being the Monster! A highly coloured account of our trip followed including a description of our appearance when we arrived at Bergen: "Judging by their beards, the Colonel and the skipper should be about the same age, but the fungus on the face is only temporary, and a symbol of the good old fashioned seafaring life on board *Caru*."

We sailed at about 1700 on Saturday evening, 11 July, and had a fine beat up the By Fjord, followed by a reach and a run on a Force 4, northerly breeze to Kviturspollen. We passed six Russian Iceland trawlers on the way, very fine looking white hulled ships accompanied by a tug, and station-keeping like men of war. Their crews waved and shouted in friendly enough fashion at our red ensign.

In Kviturspollen we anchored in among Bergen yacht club boats once more. Sunday was spent largely ashore there. We took some friends for a short sail in the afternoon and later exchanged visits with some Norwegian boats. It is their pleasant custom that strange boats visiting a port make friends and lie alongside each other. The following day was to be our last before the journey home. We sailed at 1000 with a southeasterly wind, Force 2-5, and made a stop during the day at 'Torpedo Bay', an intriguing hidden cove, so called because it was used by the resistance forces during the war. It was here that Leif Larsen, hero of the 'Shetland Bus', used to hide his MTB from the Germans, and emerge to raid their convoys. The entrance, formed by a fault in the rock, is six-feet deep by approximately 20-feet wide, quite blind from the outside, and opens into a circular cove where Larsen laid his boat alongside a steep faced rock and threw a camouflage net over her. We had an enjoyable bathe in the cove's waters, far warmer than in Ireland.

In the afternoon we beat south among the islands, and as we needed petrol for the voyage home, picked Mokster on Stolmen Island for the night. The next morning, after an hour spent checking over the standing rigging, we were off at 1000, destination the Shetlands. Word had gone round the village that we were heading across the North Sea, and most of its population turned out to wave us off – a very heart-warming gesture.

An hour took us out between the last two islets and clear of the coast. At first the northeasterly wind was too light to enable us to sail in the jumbled swell, but by 1700 it freshened and the spinnaker drew nicely. All through the night we had a magnificent run under a clear, starry sky. By 1000 the next day, however, the wind was falling light again. We got out Robin's sextant and all had some practice – I got a good meridian altitude at noon. We spoke to several Lerwick MFVs during the afternoon. They refer to Consol simply as 'the dots' and have no charts or bearings, but just know that, for example, '16 dots takes you in past Bressay.' Incidentally, these rules of thumb do not agree with the charts and several people told us that Consol is up to seven or eight miles out for the Shetlands which agreed with our own observations. By 1700 the wind was a moderate to fresh west-nor-west and we started to beat under the main and Genoa, with the rail awash and quite a lively motion below. In the early hours of the next morning we picked up the three flashes of the Sumburgh Head Light at the south end of the Shetlands. Shortly after this we saw the destroyer HMS *Diamond* which altered course and came alongside to enquire if we needed anything: then after giving us the weather forecast she continued on her way. This was much appreciated and we reckoned it a fine welcome home to British waters. At 1100 we tied up for a short stay in the basin at Lerwick just 48 hours out from the Norwegian coast.

As the weather seemed settled and the forecast was good, we decided to return home via Cape Wrath and the west coast instead of through the Canal. The 600 mile passage back would take nine days with two full and three half nights with the hook down. For half of that time there would be no wind at all, the other half a lot of rain and winds bang on our nose – the latter so persistent that it made us feel that *Caru* might at any moment metamorphose into *The Flying Dutchman*, condemned to sail in everlasting headwinds! It was quite a grind, but being three days overdue we had to keep *Caru* moving.

In this mixed bag of weather we sailed from Lerwick past the beautiful Fair Isle to the Orkneys, round Cape Wrath to the Summer Isles, and on to Flowerdale on the Gairloch. Then into the Sound of Sleat (aptly named at that stage weather-wise!) to Ardnamurchan and down the Sound of Mull, thereafter keeping outside the Garvallochs. Fully reefed we proceeded at an exhilarating pace down the west side of Scarba and Jura, tore down the Sound of Islay from whence we rejoined our old track made four weeks previously, off the east side of Islay. The North Channel crossing for the 50 or so miles to Portrush was one of the most enjoyable passages of the cruise. The sun came out and added a sparkle to the white horses around us. Gradually the coast of Ulster appeared: first Rathlin Island then the high Antrim coast, and soon we were off the Giant's Causeway close-hauled along the rocky shore. We sailed inside the Skerries, one short tack and soon after we were in the calm waters of Portrush harbour.

The highlight? The Norwegian scenery. It was everywhere magnificent and very conveniently the Hardanger Fjord – one of the largest and most beautiful of all Norway's fjords – lies on the part of the coast nearest to Scotland. The only regret was that this time one more jolly good crew was breaking up.

CHAPTER 6
Round Ireland in 'Caru'
1954

Bruce:

By 1954, Wallace's sister Jill (aged nearly 18) was already a trusted shipmate. For Jill, early adventures on Wallace's vessels were a good preparation for years of married life on a sailing-boat in the Mediterranean with her husband John Livsey and their son Andrew, who has continued to spend much of his life afloat. As she explains in her introduction, Jill and her older brothers started messing about in boats when she was a mere toddler.

Jill:

My first memory of being in a boat with Wallace was when I was invited on board the Spluto. I was four or five at the time. Bought for the household by our father, the Spluto was a ten-foot punt and both brothers, Wallace and Henry, made make-shift water paddles for her using empty spam tins. I am not sure how successful this propulsion was, as I really remember very little about the whole thing other than being absolutely terrified and promptly being placed back on dry land.

Wallace was a wonderful and kind brother. He won a classical scholarship to Shrewsbury School from where he wrote me semaphore illustrated letters about the adventures and 'expeditions' we would have in the holidays. I was six by then and longed for the day when both brothers, back from school, would thunder up the stairs to admire whatever game I had set out to show them.

We would spend the holidays, amongst other pursuits, looking for birds' nests, always careful not to go too close and frighten them away. This interest in wildlife continued throughout Wallace's life, as with most of our family. A particular bird favourite was the rare storm petrel – the sea swallow – which he delighted in spotting swooping across the waves when out sailing. He also loved plants and kept a reference book on his boats. We would enjoy looking up flowers found on the various islands we visited when we were older – some of which were rare so we were careful to take a small leaf only in such cases for identification purposes.

I often sailed with Wallace at weekends, from about the age of 12. We would leave Portrush on a Friday evening with different crews. Mostly we went over to Donegal *if the tide was right, but occasionally up to the Scottish islands; Jura, Mull, and even Iona. Of course, I was excited about sailing with him, but also apprehensive as I got very sea sick. This improved with time and a lot of singing which somehow cured me! 'Waltzing Matilda', 'We're Bound for Botany Bay', 'Speed Bonny Boat' and 'Home, Home on the Range' were boat favourites.*

Washing up was done in sea water as we carried little fresh water on board. We used to hang a bucket on a rope over the side to collect it. Never harbour water though! On several occasions we would lose the bucket with a sudden heavy jerk. Wallace remarked jokingly that perhaps one day we might run aground on lost buckets — spoons, knives and forks too! Apart from food, we never took much with us as there was so little storage room on board. It was always good, therefore, to get home, have a bath and a change of clothes!

I was 17 and just out of school when I embarked on the trip round Ireland on Caru *with Wallace and Henry and, for the first leg, Valerie Gillespie, a great friend of ours. The boat was well stocked. Numerous boxes of fruit, vegetables, eggs, loaves of bread and a great number of tins were stowed on board. I also remember when we were down to our last tin of condensed milk and a handful of potatoes just short of Cork some time later. I was for many years teased for remarking back then, "You can eat almost anything with enough tomato sauce on it!" Cooking was never my forté, then or now!*

Another memory was the comfort, or lack of it, on board. In the following log of the trip, Wallace mentions the dreaded crew rotation between three bunks and 'the hard old cabin floor'. The floor was actually a better choice than the often slightly damp fo'c'sle or narrow bunks, and usually extra blankets would fall out of the latter on to the lucky person below, so a cosy night could in fact be enjoyed in those lower reaches.

During the trip down Ireland's west coast my imagination was stirred particularly when we reached Clare Island and visited the ruined tower, house and chapel of Grace O'Malley or 'Granuaile', the sea pirate queen. I had never heard of her before that trip, but she became a heroine of mine from that moment on. She visited Elizabeth I in London and apparently neither would curtsey as they were both queens! Sailing down the west coast as she would have done was just glorious.

The magical Aran Islands are another vivid memory. We watched a fleet of sailing hookers, so seldom seen these days, bringing the islanders turf from the mainland. (Many years after this trip, while in the area on a camping holiday with some cousins, I was allowed to steer one of them over to Aran itself. The boat men had set the sail, the wind was fair and the sea reasonably calm. The hooker responded well to the tiller, but it took some considerable strength to hold her on the wind. A wonderful experience though!) Thinking about it now, the hookers, amongst other fishing vessels, were really the only other boats we saw the entire time between Portrush and Cork. The only other yacht we saw was somewhere off Kenmare. How very different to nowadays!

In the second half of the trip, having rounded Carnsore Point during the night for the easterly leg back to Portrush, Wallace roused us from our sleep to board the Blackwater Lightship. I sleepily went onboard in my bare feet and can still remember and almost feel how hot the engine room was under foot, and how bitterly cold it felt when we were being shown the refrigerator cabin. There I remember spotting a notice saying 'Fair and aisy goes far in a day' (I do agree with this!) and another above the sink saying:

> *For all of us as does the washing up,*
> *From John O'Groats to Devon -*
> *This little crumb of comfort sup,*
> *There won't be none in Heaven!*

To this day, I still feel proud to think that I might have been the first woman to circumnavigate Ireland. And Wallace – it is difficult to sum up such a man – forever generous, kind and brave, he was ready to try all things new. He had an interest in many different subjects and read widely. He was always good company, able to relate to and enjoy meeting people from many different backgrounds. He loved life to the full and we all loved being with him.

Wallace:

Caru must have made up her mind to sail round Ireland this year. Certainly neither her skipper nor crew, when we left Portrush, had the least intention of doing so. A quiet cruise down the west coast – no further south than Galway was the plan, and if the weather was bad we would lie up in Mulroy Bay. But *Caru*, always a high-stepper, had ideas of her own!

We slipped anchor at 1845 on Wednesday, 7 July, and with a moderate northeast breeze were round Malin Head an hour before midnight. Then the wind backed south-southwest and we close-hauled for the Bloody Foreland which we rounded at 1400 with the sun to greet our arrival on the west coast.

Inishsirrer Sound looks narrow on the chart, but there are a couple of leading marks (wooden posts) on the mainland which bring you in past the only hidden dangers from the north. It is a pretty spot and all around, we generally agreed, the group of islets which we passed through were the best island scenery anywhere in the west. In fact the boat port on Owey looked so attractive that we decided to anchor there on the spur of the moment and got a lift ashore in a curragh. We had an interesting walk round the island where one of the main problems is the steady disappearance of the soil as it is cut and burnt for turf. Unless checked, this is bound to make the island uninhabitable in a few years – no soil will mean no water. One of the islanders came out to see *Caru* before we pushed on and remarked that her cabin was "A wee palace!" If you know *Caru's* cabin this is quite a compliment, and her crew duly took comfort from it as their turn came around to sleep on the hard old cabin floor; there are only three bunks!

The wind had veered again south-southwest, so we reached south once more to Aranmore and anchored for the night inside Alf Island and close off 'Young Mick's Strand' – as the Admiralty chart (dated 1870) records. The next morning we motored across the sound to Rutland Harbour. Formed by a number of islands it would make a perfect pirate's lair, and the roofless herring station and dwelling houses help to give the impression that it once flourished as such.

Burtonport, a mile further east, is another deserted harbour with an abandoned railway for good measure. The magnificently built pier is still in perfect repair, and it is sad that the casting trade has passed away from it like so many west of Ireland ports. The place reminds me of photographs which have recently appeared in the yachting press of English Harbour, once Nelson's base in Antigua, now the resort of globetrotting yachtsmen who want a quiet spot to refit. There is no petrol pump, but the bus depot kindly supplied us with four gallons. We bought some groceries and departed.

The wind, now south-fresh, gave us a close-haul for Broadhaven 80 miles away. Beside Erris Head marks the start of the part of the coast we wanted to visit as well as the limit of the westing required – so an important landmark. It is also a difficult spot because of its tide rip, and could be a considerable bugbear in working your way south along the coast, so we were glad of what looked like a good opportunity to nip round. But it was not to be. The wind steadily freshened, and by late afternoon we had two reefs down and the No 2 jib out. Luckily we were still in the lee of Glen Head, so it was an easy decision to make for Glen Bay for the night. It was the strongest wind in which I have sailed *Caru*. With nine rolls in the mainsail we were still harbouring in the gusts. The rain was incessant and spray flew in sheets over the cockpit each time her bow plunged in the short, steep seas. Slowly we worked closer into the shelter and finally anchored in one fathom near the head of Glen Bay which faces due west. This was a bad spot and some lobster fishermen shortly appeared in a curragh to indicate a better anchorage in four fathoms close inside a rocky point on the south shore. It was still far from comfortable. We rolled fiercely all night and when I poked my head out at 0700 the next morning I was shaken to see that the wind had veered west and was strong; quite contrary to the forecast. A big swell with many breaking crests was rolling into the bay unchecked a few yards beyond our anchorage. Should the wind go further north we would be in imminent danger, so after the hastiest of breakfasts we got under way with two reefs in the main, the No 2 jib hoisted and the engine ticking over.

Caru was rarin' to go and never looked like having any difficulty in beating out. Only one biggish crest came on board early on. Henry, clinging to the mast having just secured the anchor, had the laugh as it missed him but soaked the three of us in the cockpit. Four or five tacks took us round Tulin Head where we freed the sheets to pass through Rathlin O'Birne Sound. The wind began to drop soon after and the reefs were rolled out as we ran east past the 2,000-foot cliffs, the highest in Europe, which fringe the entrance to Teelin. It is one of the prettiest parts I know and we enjoyed a leisurely afternoon and evening there drying clothes and sails in the sun and fishing successfully for our supper.

The next day dawned bright and clear with no wind at all. We motored out and headed west-southwest once more for Broadhaven. When the wind came it was a northwest and moderate one which gave us a pleasant reach. The swell from yesterday was about ten-foot high and shortish, but *Caru* found her way up and down it sweetly. As we drew near the Mayo coast its flat-topped, square-faced cliffs presented a starkly beautiful and unforgettable sight. It must be both the grandest cliff scenery and the most deserted part of Ireland's coast – not a house or sign of habitation to be seen for 20 miles or more, in fact all the way from Killala to Broadhaven, apart from one or two tiny villages. The oblique rays of the sun threw every nook and cove as well as the off-lying lofty pinnacles, of which there are quite a number, into strong relief of light and shadow. Pity help the ship to be thrown onto such a coast – at least there is not much fear of it happening nowadays simply because there are no ships for it to happen to. The west of Ireland is an almost deserted coast.

We made a close inspection of the Stags of Broadhaven, an isolated group of huge pyramidal rocks about four miles offshore. We were amazed to see several sheep clinging to their near vertical sides – I would love to know how their owners ever catch them. The wind piped up as we crossed Broadhaven off Erris Head. We handed the Genoa and as the sun set, the sea grew dark and angry looking. At our maximum speed we reached south for Frenchport wondering anxiously if it would provide shelter. Reports as to the protection it offers vary, and now the wind would be blowing straight into it, Force 5 and freshening. Luckily, all was well. It is much bigger inside than it looks on the chart, and the swell seemed to stop surprisingly short at the mouth. It is not a pretty place; low lying, sandy and windswept, but we spent a comfortable enough night there after what had been a very long and tiring day.

We did not feel tempted to land on the morning of 12 July, and sailed out after breakfast. Next stop was Inishkea, a deserted island inhabited only by donkeys and rabbits and a few lobstermen, who come over in their curraghs from Blacksod and sometimes spend a night or two in one of the cottages. It was warm, sunny and calm. As the tide was rising we pushed *Caru's* nose practically onto the beach before anchoring and launching the dinghy. It is a seven-foot six Prout collapsible, and two days earlier at Aranmore a sporting attempt to get all four members of the crew into it at once had ended in dismal failure – three wet pairs of trousers and loud laughter from Henry, who was lucky again – so now we do it in two trips! It would have been nice to spend all day there sunbathing, chatting to the lobstermen, looking at their curraghs and shooting an odd rabbit for the pot, but we had to cut these activities rather short and speed away to catch the tide up Achill Sound at the Bull's Mouth. There is a pleasant looking pub at the narrows too, but the five-knot flood unfortunately forbade us to stop.

Once through the Bull's Mouth we anchored for the night in the pool south of the bridge – The Bags – where there is about two fathoms at low water Spring Tide which is worth knowing as from the chart you get the impression that it all dries out. Sweeney's shop, where we proceeded to store up, may well be described the 'Harrods of the West'; they supply anything from a ballet skirt to a second-hand coffin, and while we did not actually require either of these items, we did make good a lot of gaps in our equipment.

The next morning we had to sail at 0500 when there would be enough water to get out. Henry and I worked *Caru* slowly down the channel with the lead going all the way, while Jill and Val snored below. At 0700 we anchored off Granuaile's Tower at Kildavnet for breakfast and a warm up. It is a lovely spot, but all the high ground was blanked out by the mist – a pity to be missing the scenery. After a rather nerve-wracking try to follow the coast west, we turned back and anchored in the lee of Achill Beg. It then occurred to the planning department that we had two relatives in the district, and it was an ideal day for fulfilling social engagements ashore, so westward the course to Mallaranny. Visibility improved a fraction, we were sheltered from the swell and the coast was clean so it was not hard to get there on a fast reach, and at 1230 we anchored off the pier.

At 1500, still in bad visibility and now accompanied by uninterrupted rain, we set off for Newport. The islands along the way are dullish as islands go; round-topped grassy knolls, here and there a ruined house, but not many distinguishing features. It was one of the heaviest and longest downpours of rain I remember. The air itself seemed liquid and no oilskin a match for it.

We reached Newport at 1900 at high tide. After some inquiries we decided to dry out on the mud in mid channel. The alternative is to do so alongside the wall. There is definitely nowhere close to the town with more than a couple of feet at low water. It is an interesting and unusual old port. It is tree-ringed and very 'inland' in appearance, but with fine stone jetties and a vast warehouse, now derelict, overlooking them. What a lot of laborious kedging and warping must have gone into bringing the old sailing coasters up her. So far, as enquiries elicited, no yacht had visited the place for 20 years or more. It would be interesting to hear of who last did so.

We had a first class dinner with most hospitable Uncle Willie and Aunt Zelie, and a dry out ashore, but had to be off all too early next morning to catch the ebb. Needless to say it was raining and cold as we motored down-channel to drop the hook off Inishmore for breakfast. The wind rose rapidly in the west to a Force 6 while we ate, so we put off sailing for Clare Island and fetched across to better shelter in Inishgowla Bay. At around 1400 it seemed to ease, so with two reefs and the No 2 jib we beat slowly out to the island which was keeping most of the swell out of Clew Bay, wondering if it would provide a safe anchorage for the night. Luckily it did. The harbour is very pretty with its clean white sandy bottom, all dry at low water, and the bay provides good anchorage in the west wind. The castle which overlooks it must have been a fine base for Granuaile, when her pirate galleys ruled the coast in the days of Queen Elizabeth I.

The next morning we hired a pony and trap to drive around the island. The abbey has a very beautiful stone arch and is well worth a visit. The population is dwindling here but on Inishturk, ten miles further south, we were told the reverse is the case and that there is a housing shortage! We walked out to see the watchtower at the southwest end of the island – it is a fine square stone structure, one of a large number spaced out along the west and northwest coasts of Ireland – in most cases visible one from the next. When they were built or for exactly what purpose I have never definitely heard. This one, judging by the size of its windows, must have been in use in the glazing era. It may have been for Coastguards or, quite the reverse, a pirate look-out, or just a link in a signalling system. It would be interesting to hear the story.

In the afternoon we sailed south once more to Killary Bay (Ireland's 'fjord') and had a fine spinnaker run up its eight-mile length; what a pleasant change to be out of the swell. The mountains rise 2,000 feet on either side in steep, almost unbroken slopes and there is deep water right up to the shores, so it does quite closely resemble the upper reaches of the Hardanger Fjord which *Caru* visited last summer, though built to about half-scale. Finding its entrance was a bit of a worry in patchy visibility with all the hill-tops hidden, but once we had the black lump of Frehil positively identified and passed from the inside it was not so difficult.

The half-tide and sunken rocks, labelled 'breakers', in which this part of the coast abounds, look deadly in the chart, but are not nearly so bad in practice. They are about as easy to spot as a low lying rock which never covers, so if you keep a reasonable lookout they need not cause any worry.

Friday night was spent at Leenane. The next morning, after beating down to the mouth of the bay in mist and drizzle, we anchored in close to the south shore and debated for some time if it was wise to go out. The south to southwest strong wind meant shelter from the land all but the last three miles or so to Inishbofin, so when visibility improved about midday we nosed out. The leading marks, faced on the seaward side with glazed white tiles, show up a long way and took us easily out on a close-haul past the dangers. Soon we picked up Inish Lyon, then Bofin itself, and only the last mile beating southwest to the harbour entrance was rough although spray had been flying steadily over the cockpit for most of the four-hour passage.

We stayed in Bofin Harbour, weather-bound for two days, along with half a dozen or so fishing boats. The gas bottle ran out quite unexpectedly and our baby Primus packed up so we had to buy a big second-hand one from the very kind Mrs Day at the hotel, who then went on to contact the local priest who in turn organised two of his lads to get a gas cylinder 'for some young Protestants'! (Mrs Day, an upright and attractive figure, would welcome us 50 years later in her home in Inishbofin, beside the hotel that was built by her sons.)

We had really meant to turn for home at this juncture but decided we must take a closer look at the Aran Islands having been stuck near them for so long. We slipped at 0545 in a light, southwest wind and a bit of a swell, and after a 40 mile passage reached Inis Mór at 1500. Here we took to horse and trap once more for a visit to Dún Aengus, the fantastic Cyclopean fort built on the edge of a sheer 300-foot cliff. We also saw a crios, the traditional island woollen belt, being woven in a farm house by what must be the crudest method practiced anywhere in the world today. This is no slur on the weaver who was most informative and interesting. When we got back to Kilronan, Joe Doyle, the lifeboat coxswain, and described at Inishbofin as the 'finest man in England, Ireland, Scotland or Wales', had a real old Irish tea waiting for us in his house.

Perhaps the most magical thing about the island is the fleet of sailing hookers which bring turf over to it daily from Cashla Bay, Roundstone, and other Connemara ports. There are still half a dozen trading regularly, engineless gaff cutter rigs with two men for a crew. A look at their masts makes you wonder whether the Éire Post Office misses any telegraph poles now and then. The standing rigging must be quite superfluous (as you could tell from a look at their condition!). They run from 11 to 16 tons, about 35' x 11'8" x 6'8" being typically short and broad with very hollow bows. The hooker is said to be exceedingly lively in a sea and safe in all conditions, except when running deep, when they are sometimes pooped due to their lean hollow runs. Unfortunately they are now all old boats, and no new ones are likely to be built. Some calculations from the chart before we turned in showed that it was 250 miles home to Portrush and 190 miles on to Cork. Getting another holiday long enough to bring her home from the latter in August would be difficult, so we decided it better be 'Home James.'

The next morning we sailed at 0800 and had headed out past the buoy for

Wallace in Royal Navy uniform, circa 1946
(Wallace Clark Collection)

Zamorin off Culdaff, Inishowen, Co Donegal, 1951
(Wallace Clark Collection)

A Norwegian anchorage: *Caru* in Bergen,
1953
('Morgenavisen')

Caru off Carrickabraghy, Inishowen, Co Donegal, 1954
(Wallace Clark Collection)

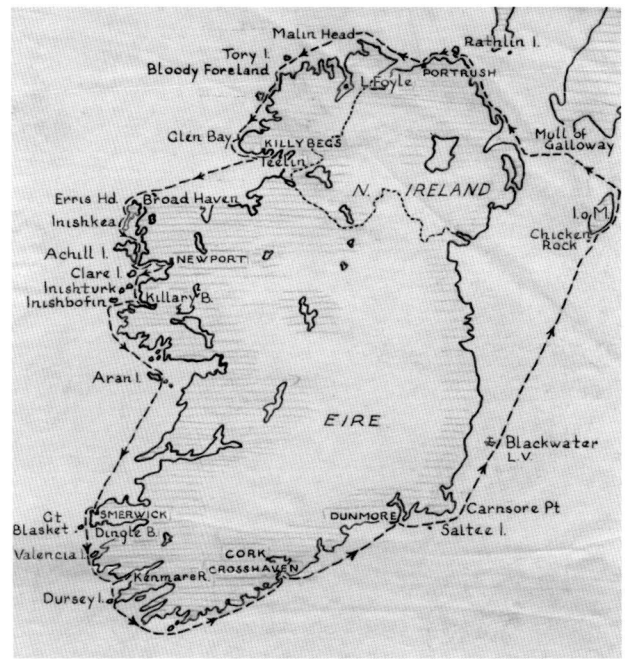

Circumnavigating Ireland: Map of *Caru's* voyage,
1954

Jill and Henry Clark and Val Gillespie, off Kerry on the *Caru*
round Ireland voyage, 1954
(Jill Livsey Collection)

Some 'Wild Geese' in the cabin,
sailing home from Rathlin, 1956
L to R: Wallace, Marcus McCausland,
Mike Ross & Mike Villiers-Stuart
(Wallace Clark Collection)

June aboard *Wild Goose* on the Midi Canal, France, 1961
(Wallace Clark Collection)

Miles and Bruce, circa 1969
(Wallace Clark Collection)

Jim Boyd, Iona curragh builder and Wallace,
Carrickfin, Co Donegal
(Alistair Jameson Collection)

The Iona Curragh Voyage, 1963
(Alistair Jameson Collection)

St Columba's Day, Balnahard Bay, North Colonsay,
Iona Curragh Voyage, 1963
(Alistair Jameson Collection)

Iona: giving thanks for a safe arrival, 1963
(Alistair Jameson Collection)

Fingal's Cave, Staffa
(Pastel painting by Ros Harvey, 2009)

Slyne when the wind seemed to come out of the north. "To hell with more beating," we said, "let's go south." And that was that. In fact when we got through the sound and clear of the island the wind was south of west and we were close-hauled all day on our course to round the Dingle Peninsula, but nobody mentions that! Smerwick Harbour appeared at long last, a niche in the massive Dingle Mountains, and we thankfully got the hook down at about midnight – 60 miles on our way. It is too big a place for a small yacht, and with the swell rolling in and high mountains all around, we felt rather like a solitary pea in a very large saucepan.

We had an early start the next morning, and after three tacks out of the bay we really did have a free wind. There was a most confused, steep sea and swell at the entrance to Blasket Sound. In a westerly wind, Force 5, Jill and I nursed *Caru* through it as best we could and were glad when the hungry black rocks of Sybil Point slid astern after having been all too close leeward. We anchored for breakfast in the lee of the Great Blasket. Unfortunately there was too much of a swell and popple for more than one at a time to have landed in our punt, so we did not bother.

After we got underway, the wind veered and gave us a really enjoyable spinnaker run across Dingle Bay, past Valentia Island, Puffin Island, and so to Ballinskelligs Bay. The following swell was a big one, and at times an odd monster came rolling up under us 20-feet high at least and not long, so that the switch back effect was quite breathtaking when you looked astern. We turned into Kenmare River past Two Head Island, and had a fast reach up to Parknasilla in perfect conditions – a bright blue, sparkling sea and sunshine. This is without doubt the most beautiful of all Ireland's bays – as fine as any in the world. The proportion and colouring of Magillicuddy's Reeks in the background, the shores varying between rock, pasture and woodland, the many sheltered coves and boat forts along its length – we could go on and on, but just come and see it for yourself some day.

High water was at 1900, so we climbed into Number Ones underway and were able to sail alongside the Hotel pier and step ashore for dinner feeling somewhat aristocratic. The next day Henry left us to assist at Drogheda Regatta, and Jill, Val and I took *Caru* on the last 100 miles to Cork in just under 24 hours; a fast reach down Kenmare River, some baffling winds in Dursey Sound, all the rest a lovely spinnaker run in warm but grey weather and a smooth sea. During the night brilliant phosphorescence foamed all around us as we sped east at near our maximum speed at times, and one by one the headlands went past until finally we turned to beat into Crosshaven. And not too soon either; we had all but run out of food. A rushed two hours followed during which we arranged to leave *Caru* with Jack Keating of Battridge's Boatyard, gathered up a few clothes and dashed ashore to get the train home.

Three weeks later at midnight, on 12 August, we arrived back. Henry had driven a fresh crew of four of us in his 10 HP Ford the 300 miles from Malin Head over the course of a day. At least the close confined experience made *Caru* seem spacious in comparison. The team was sister Jill, Ian Martin, Euan Storey and myself.

A quiet weeknight gathering was in progress at the Royal Munster Yacht Club. "Not a party," as members assured us, "just a few people gathered up to meet the RORC boats arriving in from the Brigham Race." Anyway, the Club was ablaze with light and you could not get near it for cars. There were dancing girls, a number of old friends and plenty of Guinness. I wish quiet weeknights were like that at Portrush!

We sailed next morning at 1100. And yes, you guessed it, it was raining. Once outside Crosshaven the sun appeared and we set the spinnaker. But the sea built up quickly from then on in, and the west-southwest wind increased to a good Force 5, perhaps 6 in the gusts. Not long after we had put a reef in the mainsail, the spinnaker, an old one, well and truly split. Euan and Ian, the new chums, had a trying job gathering its flailing pieces then lowering the mainsail which was nastily fouled, the top batten having come half way out and in the process wedged itself between two shrouds. Meanwhile a trailing spinnaker guy got caught around the propeller screw – the engine was not running at the time, but the declutched propeller rotating as we sailed had picked up the rope hard enough to jam itself. Not that it mattered for the moment, but just one more complication. However, things were sorted out at last, and with the mainsail reset and the Genoa boomed out, we had a fast run to Dunmore East where we put in for the night and Ian dived over the side to clear the screw, which he did in no time at all.

With a light west wind and sunshine the next day we sailed for the Saltees but couldn't linger as we had only five days for the 320 miles Cork to Portrush leg and so had to push on. At 0600 next morning we could be found reaching past the Blackwater Lightship having rounded Carnsore

Point during the night. The watch on the lightship deck gave us a wave and we decided to pay them a visit. A moment later we tied up alongside. *Caru* rode quite easily beside it, and Jill and Ian, aroused from their slumbers, wondered what on earth was going on. We were swiftly haled down to the mess deck and while 14 full hammocks swayed gently above us enjoyed an excellent cup of tea followed by the 'grand tour' of the ship – all in the true traditions of Irish Lights' hospitality. It was a good start to the day which was passed well off-shore close-reaching with the main and Genoa en route for the Isle of Man.

Around dusk the sea grew a bit 'gurly' and appetites for supper diminished. It looked like we were in for a rough night, but fortunately the weather was only bluffing, and soon fell light. The moonlight was spectacular and the air warm until two or three, but how cold it got then. The Chicken Rock Light was a most welcome sight when it appeared fine on the starboard bow at dawn. Four more hours took us into Port St Mary for a hearty breakfast followed by a sound sleep at anchor in the shelter of the pier. We set off again at 1600 to enjoy a fast reach right along the east coast of the island. The conditions were ideal with a whole-sail breeze off the land and dead calm water enabling us to get a good impression of the whole island which none of us had visited before. The strung-out lights of Ramsay looked most inviting in the dusk, but we still had to press on.

After rounding the point of Ayre we could just about lay the Mull of Galloway close-hauled. The wind died fairly soon after that and most of the night was spent under engine. I was standing out of watches as skipper, and was not called out once which made a pleasant change. By breakfast we were close off the County Down coast at Ballyferris point. The tide was just turning foul, so we got right in close to work the eddy. We made Muck Island by the end of the foul tide at midday and at the end of the next north going ebb we were just around Fair Head. We were now only 18 miles from home so decided to put in at Rathlin Island for a few hours.

It was just after dusk as we slipped into Church Bay and tied up alongside the north pier. Brigadier Gage and his family were as hospitable as ever. When we came back to the pier at midnight, the warm air and moonlight, almost as bright as day, made it seem a thorough waste of time to go to sleep, so to the notes of Euan's squeeze-box, and no doubt the consternation of the islanders, we made a fair attempt at an eightsome reel on the shore after which Euan climbed the mast for sheer *joie de vivre*. This latter feeling was not quite so obvious when the alarm clock went off three hours later at 0400, dragging us from our bunks as from wells of treacle to catch the west-going tide. There was an east wind to which we set in turn the No 1 jib, Genoa, and spinnaker to reach Portrush at 0700, just on schedule, for I was due back at work at 0900!

It had been a most enjoyable five days, with good breezes, great company and hardly a drop of rain. The round trip had taken 20 days, 18 of them sailing, and amounted to about 870 miles; a bit of a rush, but *Caru* had the bit firmly between her teeth and there was just no holding her!

CHAPTER 7
A 'Wild Goose' Joins the Fleet
1956

Have you watched the swallow building?
Have you seen the wheatear mating?
Have you lain alone to hear the wild goose cry?
(After Rudyard Kipling's 'The Feet of the Young Men')

Bruce:

This chapter needs no human presenter. Wild Goose *introduces herself. Having changed boats frequently in his earliest yachting days, Wallace and later his family would hold tenaciously to* Wild Goose *for four happy decades. Finally this grande dame of the Celtic (and by then Russian) waterways had an unfortunate, but luckily not permanent, encounter with the ocean floor when turning into the mouth of the river Bann, in 1998. But Wallace's 42 years aboard the* Goose *were the prime of his sailing career. My mother (who married in 1957) would say of* Wild Goose, "Wallace has had her longer than he's had me!"

Wallace:

It adds tremendously to the interest of sailing to change now and then. After four seasons of excellent service, I sold *Caru* to Ray Clarke of Derry in December 1955 and bought *Wild Lone II* from Mervyn Henry of Coleraine around the same time. I renamed her *Wild Goose*, after my love for the wildfowl of the Donegal coast in Ireland. She is a ten-ton, shoal draft Bermudan yawl, 25'6" x 28'0" x 9'4" x 4'10", with a Parsons Prawn engine, designed by Maurice Griffiths and built by Harry King of Pin Mill, Sussex, in 1936. She spent the winter on the Bann at Coleraine and was pulled up at Portstewart at the beginning of March and a new doghouse added under the competent supervision of Dan McClelland, master joiner. *Wild Goose* was launched at 0700 on Saturday 14 April. The mast was stepped at noon seven miles away at Coleraine Quay, the nearest crane, and so to moorings at Portrush. During May and June we had a number of weekend cruises; several times to Culdaff, twice to Rathlin Island, once to Trawbreaga Bay and once to Gigha off Kintyre. During this time *Wild Goose* taught me a bit about using two masts.

A hard lesson was learned as we crossed Trawbreaga Bar on Sunday morning, 3 June. We had gone into the bay on the flood the previous evening in flat calm. We had learned that high water slack tide was around 1000 the following morning, but as everything seemed quiet, sunny and windless, we thought little of being an hour late getting underway, which meant we only reached the bar when a considerable ebb was already running, perhaps three to four knots in the narrows of the channel. As we cleared the narrows the bar presented a horrid sight. Masses of surf leapt into the air all over the channel, which is about 150 yards wide, with few gaps, and heavy and continuous surf breaking on the rocks to the south and on Lag Spit which guards the bar on the north. The dinghy, which I had failed to put on deck, capsized. We turned, under engine, but found the ebb stream was by then too strong to allow us to re-enter. Short of abandoning the little boat, all we could do was turn once more and try our luck. We passed through three successive combing waves, the breaking face of which appeared about four-feet high and over which *Wild Goose* rose easily and quite unchecked. The way ahead then looked clear and I had just said we were safely through when the daddy of them, incredibly short, got up ahead of us. We must have been on the shallowest part of the bar – about 10-11 feet of water at that state of the tide – and what looked like an ordinary swell approaching suddenly piled up as the ground shoaled under it. The breaking face was, I estimated, six to eight feet high as it bore down on us, and all the comparatively level water on which we lay seemed to be creamed into white froth. Just what one sees between successive small breakers near the shore. I suppose the top four feet of the wave came unchecked over the bow and swept clean over us aft. The force was sufficient to catch the sliding hatch, which was open where it overhangs the doghouse, and tearing it clean out of its slides, threw the whole hatch into the cockpit. Davy Lee, standing grasping the mizzen rigging, was hit on the chest by heavy water but held on. The boat was thrown bodily back three or four feet as if on her haunches and the tiller plucked clean out of my hands as she moved rapidly astern. However, since we must have met the wave absolutely square, she showed no tendency to broach or slew either way. And as the good old Parsons Prawn chugged away, we slowly gathered headway, and borne along by the strong ebb, we were clear of the danger in a few minutes. There was little wind and we had no sail set. I doubt if it would have helped in any way. After this experience, the best advice I can give those about to cross bars in such conditions is DON'T! But if the engine had swamped or failed at the last big wave,

I think we would still have been all right as the momentum of the ebb would probably have carried us through, clear of the danger, before the next breaker. You may ask why the hatch was open: we had a landsman on board who had gone into the cabin for shelter, so I had left it open to maintain communication.

An hour earlier and probably two hours later the bar would have been flatter. I have since discovered that it is the first hour of the ebb which is worst at Trawbreaga, not the third and fourth as one might expect.

The early plan had been to take *Wild Goose* to France but shore complications prevented this and the almost equally attractive alternative of a two-week run down the west coast of Ireland emerged instead.

The crew was a fine assortment. Michael Ross of RNIYC was on board throughout. Paddy McCorkell of Derry came for the first four days when his place was taken by Harry Woodhead, rector of Malin, who briefly swapped his dog-collar for our dog-house. The idea was to keep going fairly hard as far as the Roundstone and Aran Island area, spend some time day-sailing thereabouts and then come home, seeing as many of the islands as possible both ways. The weather was about average. I believe three bad days to one good in summer is the local rule in the west.

We slipped from Portrush at 2200 on Friday, 29 June, in a southwesterly wind, Force 5, and had a fine reach northwest to Malin Head. At 0600 the next day a fierce squall blew out of the Swilly, gusting probably to Force 7 and made us roll down a lot of mainsail. It would have been most unpleasant round the Bloody Foreland and we were all very tired, so we put into Portnablagh for breakfast and a rest at around 1100. The centre of a depression passed very close to us during the day and there was a curious forecast of 'winds between southeast and north, Force 2-7'. The strong south wind showed no signs of dropping, so in the afternoon we shifted further up the bay to Downings and after a tough job getting properly tied up, managed to spend a comfortable night alongside. We were off at 0700 the next morning with a fair southeasterly wind which blew us rapidly round to the Bloody Foreland. There the wind kindly backed north, dropped to about Force 3 and the sun came out – as did the rum. There were some worrying minutes dodging the Ballyconnell breakers which are unmarked and lie right on the course south, about half a mile off Gola Island. One of them threw a growling mass of foam out of the calm blue sea as we passed. As navigator, I tried to look as if that was just what I had expected, but I doubt if the crew were convinced.

We ploughed on south by southwest towards Erris Head. It looked as if we would be lucky and get round first time, which can often be the main bugbear when working south along the west coast. But at 1930 the forecast was 'backing west and increasing to Force 7 by morning'. We might just have made Broadhaven before it blew up, we might not; the wind might increase earlier than expected and the prospect of being close hauled for a not altogether easy landfall in the dark in a Force 7 with such a big swell running, was not inviting. On the other hand, it might never blow up at all; the weather, as Claude Worth remarks, likes bluffing; it can bluff the Met Office as much as me or you. The clouds thicken, the glass drops, the wind starts to rise; then a few hours later everything brightens and you congratulate yourself on not having sought shelter unnecessarily. What would you do? We turned tail for Killybegs. Looking back, we were right.

At that time, with the weather unsettled and little time to spare, it seemed disappointing to throw away 40-50 miles of hard westing and run into a large, deep Donegal bay, not all that well provided with satisfactory harbours. But in fact we had three or four of the best days of the cruise in there and saw lots of worthwhile people and places.

On Monday, 2 July, a big smart fishing vessel, the *Morana*, kindly wirelessed back a report of wind and sea conditions. In spite of their encouraging words about 'just a wee summer breeze' we found it too tough going to close-haul for Erris Head, and ran off east once more for Mullaghmore. The next day we sailed to Inishmurray against a light west wind and went ashore in hot sun. There were fascinating Christian relics. An air of long abandonment also enveloped the houses on the south shore. The island had been evacuated about six years ago. In every house was a litter of pictures, furniture, books and mattresses, many of which must have been in good condition when left. It is said that stilling poteen was the main industry and highly lucrative, so that perhaps there were a number of unwilling evacuees!

We reached Rosses Point, Sligo Harbour, at 1900 for dinner ashore, and the first crew change. With Harry Woodhead and minus Paddy we sailed again early the following morning and plugged solidly west all day, mainly in a flat calm and unceasing rain. Downpatrick Head, though only 115 feet in height, sticks in my memory as one of the most impressive Irish promontories. Curiously enough the 2,000-foot, cliff-like slopes of Slieve League on the north side of Donegal Bay do not look anything out of the ordinary from close to. Downpatrick's black cliffs drop sheer into deep water and looked very imposing as we motored close under them; their formation makes long narrow ledges on which hundreds of guillemots stood like guardsmen on parade.

As we reached Erris Head it blew up from the north and we had an exhilarating run south through Eagle Island Sound, jumbled and tide riven as usual, just reaching Frenchport as it grew dark. We beat out the next morning and reached south on a pleasant west wind. In Inishkea Sound we met another yacht – quite an event in 'The West'. She turned out to be *Harrier* of the RCC, sailed by John Ives, and through a shouted conversation we found we were acquainted on paper at least.

We rounded Achill Head again in a mighty jumble of swell and tide, and ran into Keem Bay hoping to see some shark fishing but were about three days too late. The bay was quite deserted with only one or two upturned curraghs on the beach and no inhabited houses in sight. So on again for Inishturk, 15 miles away. It was as fine a sail as one could ask for; a whole-sail breeze, bouncing beam swell, the sea fleshed with white horses and gleaming in the bright sun, the superb silhouettes of the Mayo and Connemara mountains for a background, and an unknown island ahead.

Turk was perhaps the most isolated of the islands which were still inhabited. It is comparatively large in area, steep and rocky, and only supports 15 families. After a walk ashore, we spent a comfortable night in the bay on the east side.

The next day we made an early morning visit to an interesting character – a young Dubliner spending four weeks on Caher Island. Whatever his reason for being alone on the island, he did not disclose it, but showed us round his kingdom with all its religious relics, seeming glad of company. We reached Bofin for lunch, intending a two-hour stop, but met so many friends from my two previous visits that it proved quite impossible to leave. Bofin is quite prosperous by island standards. I have never visited a small community – about 60 families – with so many characters, all individual, but united in their friendliness. Take 'Squire' O'Halloran, the pilot; Pateen Clohert, who steered us into the quay; or hotelier Margaret Day, who gave a warm welcome to my son Bruce, leading an international party of 40 Christian history buffs, in 2009. Then there was Sandy Baird who came for the weekend a few years earlier and stayed. Other characters include Michael Schofield, descendant of one of the garrison Cromwell abandoned, who knows where storm petrels nest on High Island; Patrick

Concannon, real life hero of a great gale that passed into literary fame, and Father O'Malley, who offered strong refreshment and fine conversation.

The next day we set off once more bound for Roundstone. After a careful look-see we decided to go through Joyce's Sound Pass inside Slyne. The wind was light, but there was rather too much swell for the job. You need to be careful not to take the nearby Blind Sound for Joyce's. Perhaps we were on our mettle, because nearby lies the Clark Rock. Did some shady forebear of mine drown there?

The next few days passed pleasantly, in more leisurely style than the passage down. We had a full week without rain. Cashel, Cashla, and Kilkieran were visited, and we passed through Beala Dangan, stemming about four knots of tide through the narrow piers of the swing bridge, and had a delightful day sail to Kilronan on Aran in company with *Davillaun*, Colonel Berridge's fine nine-tonner. We had five on board having recently been joined by the Tony McCleerys, *père et fils*, of Strangford.

On Wednesday, Tony Senior, Mike and I made a chilly 0600 start from Golam Harbour and watched a smoky red, beautiful, but rather ominous sunrise as we ran out the narrow entrance and east past Macdara's Island to Roundstone. There we had a second breakfast at 1000 and Tony Senior left for the long drive home to Ringhaddy.

We rounded Slyne and anchored in Bofin harbour once more in the early evening. The next day it blew hard from the south and southeast, which would have meant a rough sea at the harbour mouth, but a fine run once underway. We put off sailing, influenced by the Bofin hospitality, and duly paid for wasting a breeze with a lot of windward slogging later. We sailed eventually at 0530 the next morning to begin the four day trek to Portrush; the wind had eased to Force 5 or so, and we ran through Inishshark Sound and straight on past Achill, stopping just before lunch at Inishglora. This low-lying island about two miles off shore has a traditional link with Saint Brendan, who sailed to America. You can see his bed with a stone bracket just above, which might have been designed for a hand bearing compass. Storm petrels now nest in the walls of his tiny cell. In one spot a coat would have covered four nests hidden among the boulders, and the parents seemed in no hurry to leave. A party of fishermen were on the island, and with typical local generosity, gave us two lobsters.

We had thought of landing on Eagle Island, but although Inishglora was calm, Eagle was unapproachable, so we pushed on and hove-to for supper in the entrance to Broadhaven before setting out on the 100-mile leg to windward to the Bloody Foreland. In winds of Force 4-5 this took 34 hours and we reached Tory Island at about 0900 the following morning, having split our mainsail in the dark, under the cliffs of Aranmore four hours earlier. The job of furling the bits was illuminated unpleasantly by the harsh rays of the lighthouse above us, and each revolution showed up in turn the jagged rocky pinnacles at the base of the cliffs close to windward. With a foul tide and under jib and mizzen only, it seemed to take an age to work past Aranmore and its outlying dangers.

I had not seen my Tory friends for a couple of years, so the welcome was warm. There was an enjoyable dance in the schoolhouse, raised in our honour. Dawn was breaking as this ended and we sailed straight away at 0400 to windward once more, Portrush bound. It had been a wonderful cruise, thanks to Mike Ross's camaraderie, plus Harry Woodhead's expertise in Irish which endeared him to many people. Behind Harry's amiable manner, there was a deep spirituality. An Anglican with a universal Christian spirit, Harry was living proof that proficiency in Gaelic lore and language is not the monopoly of any group.

CHAPTER 8
Short Cut to the Sun

Bruce:

Despite the constraints imposed by shortish holidays and children (I arrived in 1958 and my brother in 1960), Wallace was ingenious in devising ways to have sailing time in relatively exotic waters. The help of Bernard was crucial. In 1961 Wallace took **Wild Goose** through the inland waterways of France to the Riviera, where the beloved vessel would spend two winters under Bernard's care. This chapter is introduced by my mother June Clark. Her memories were still crystal-clear half a century later. Bernard has some lively addenda.

June:

Negotiating those French locks was hard work but was worth it. It enabled Wallace and me to have the first of many enjoyable journeys to the sailing grounds of the Mediterranean, from the Riviera to the Aegean. Working through the canals allowed me to enjoy the countryside, practise my French and taste gourmet food. The pleasantest moments were in the early morning and late afternoon when the sun was not too strong. At one point in our French canal journeys, Wallace had to return for a business meeting so he left me and my brother John to navigate the locks. Then John and I realised that neither of us understood the engine; each of us had assumed the other did. But somehow we worked it out and Wallace was pleased with our progress when he returned.

I remember spotting Princess Grace at our restaurant in Carcassonne. I was better than Wallace at noticing celebrities. I also recall the time I was told to swim to the river bank with a rope. A group of men sitting at a nearby café were surprised to see me emerging from the water and offered to help. Wallace's notes do not make clear whether the locals were happy to manhandle me out of the water, or happy to help with the rope. Perhaps both. When we finally reached the Mediterranean, Wallace and Bernard enjoyed some hair-raising sails, while I stayed on dry land where I benefited from the hospitality and advice of Bernard's mother and his wife Marcelle. For example, when I had a tummy upset, they prescribed jam and it worked. They were very kind. On a winter's night in Ireland 50 years later, I still enjoy thinking about the brilliant light and bright blue seas of the Mediterranean.

Wallace:

"The grand object of all travelling," said Dr Johnson, "is to see the shores of the Mediterranean." Our aspirations to do so under sail had always been thwarted by the time limit of a three-week holiday. But it can be done. The magic carpet is the Midi Canal, which brings the south coast of France within a 300-mile ditch-crawl of Bordeaux. The margin for breakdown or bad weather was estimated at only two or three days.

The canals posed many unfamiliar problems. "You'll need the three most useless objects afloat," we were told, "...a step ladder, a push bike and an umbrella." Another bit of advice was to check the length of the mast which would be laid along the deck. "If it sticks out over the stern it's bound to get broken." All good advice, as we later discovered, but luckily the more fearsome warnings apply only to the main canals. In the Midi the locks are so small that sharing with barges is quite exceptional. But we needed to make a gangplank, awning and icebox, and to carry bosun's stores for three weeks, for these items are expensive in France. The driving force behind the search for answers to practical questions was my wife, June. Without her enthusiasm, at times when I was tempted to give up, we should never have made it. Vital help also came from Bernard Felix.

The Midi system begins at Bordeaux and consists of the Canal Lateral à la Garonne as far as Toulouse, and Canal du Midi from there to Sette. There are a number of branches including one joining the Rhone at Arles and leading on to Marseilles. That branch has 118 locks, many of them double or treble, is 300 miles in length, and rises 600 feet. Draught is what worries most people. *Wild Goose* draws a nominal five feet. We could remove the six cwt of inside ballast, but even without this, the extra stores would put her down a couple of inches and the transition to fresh water two more. For the first 150 miles there is no problem for this part of the canal is comparatively modern and over two metres in depth. The southern part, however, is the oldest waterway in France, built in 1670, and is officially listed as suitable for vessels drawing from one to six metres maximum.

In fact, as we went through drawing five feet and five inches we had no trouble. Five years ago British yachts were a rarity, but in 1960 some 27 went through and 24 the year after. We needed a good crew: Mike, who had sailed everything from corvettes to clipper ships and had doubtful stories about them all; Bruce Bolton, a Cambridge undergraduate, who had flair as a cook; and Alan Parsons, an Oxford-trained lawyer from Wales who taught us an unprintable, unpronounceable national toast.

A great moment came at 2100 one evening off Brittany when Stiff and Creach, those two curiously named Ouessant Lights, blinked out clear as bells abeam and eight miles to leeward. It is a foggy corner normally, but our luck was in and we sailed on in ideal conditions. All night we romped along down the path of the moon on a broad reach in a sea sufficiently jumbled to be interesting but devoid of menace and with enough shipping to keep the helmsman awake, although nothing remotely frightening. A passenger liner passing close by got me so enthralled, taking in the lights and music, that I forgot to look out for her bow wave and was brought to order by furious yells from the watch as water sluiced over the bow and through the forehatch.

For the second night, as I turned in at 0200, the full moon was winking through the scuttles. What fun it is sailing under her benign light. It is well worth planning a passage to suit it; the work on deck and navigating are much easier, and there is a lot of truth in the old Spanish proverb which says: 'The moon calms all she looks down on.' If it is blowing when the full moon rises, the wind and sea almost always drop away very considerably. Just as the moon moves water masses to produce tides, so it must influence moist air masses, though in a subtler way which is not yet understood.

A five-knot vessel can make Bordeaux in one tide as the flood runs in for nearly nine hours. Conditions were almost ideal with moderate visibility and a very slight swell, which was breaking gently on the shallow banks. We slipped past the sandy hook of Point de la Coubre and picked our way without difficulty past the flat, unattractive shores on which the chart shows famous names like Graves, Médoc, and St Julien. The log read like a wine list.

An engine stoppage off Pauillac at 1700 just cost us our tide to Bordeaux. We lost about three-quarters of an hour tracing the overheating trouble to an airlock in the water pump. Blaye seemed the best bet for the night, although it meant leaving the buoyed channel and crossing to the north side of the estuary which was about two-miles wide at this point. We crept across with extreme care, the lead line in constant use and helped by shouted instructions from a dredger. We tied up for the night alongside a tubby, comic-looking river ferry, and it was after midnight when we turned in.

We awoke at 0430 the next morning to start at first light and kept close to the high north bank initially. Approaching the junction of the Dordogne and Garonne, the current was at its fiercest and boiled round the buoys as we sped past the great refinery at Bec d'Ambès and into the quieter waters of the Garonne.

We tied up alongside on the south side a quarter-mile below the bridge of Bordeaux city at 0730, just as the ebb began; an uncomfortable berth but convenient for the Customs, cranes and shops. Just above us lay a square rigger, her sails so beautifully stowed that at first sight we thought her yards were bare. Astern of her were two white-hulled escort vessels and we soon discovered that she was the *Eagle*, an American Coastguard sail-training barque.

The Customs arrived at 0830 and were courteous; they sealed up our duty-free stores after seeing that we had ample for the rigours of the next ten days inland. A crane would cost NF33 for one hour. This seemed a lot, so while the crew slacked off the rigging and unshipped the life lines I visited the *Niger Palm*, the only British ship in port, heading home after three months off West Africa. The mate agreed to lend us a derrick and by lunchtime, after a hard morning's work, both sticks were down on the crutches. A pleasant hour of beer drinking with cadets and bosun followed. We were showered with presents and African souvenirs by sailors who were surprised to see yachtsmen work so hard!

The local bargemen were helpful. We soon found one due to leave the next morning and tied up to her for the night. We started out at first light, but after the first quarter of a mile a thick fog descended and we had to come back and wait until it cleared at 0900. It was a pretty voyage, full of interest, and a pleasant breeze blew across the river. There were many dredgers, a fair amount of barge traffic and numerous rod and net fishermen. Some operate by lowering a huge dish-shaped net into the river and then raising it rapidly with a hand winch.

The flood runs for only four hours and we had missed most of it, but the ebb did not amount to more than a knot or two. The channel invariably followed the outside of the bends and the pilotage did not seem unduly difficult. The high, steel railway bridge just before Castets is unmistakable and we turned into one of the twin locks just beyond it. Once we reached the upper level and were screened by trees from the breeze, the heat descended as if a furnace door had been opened. We hastened to rig the awning.

The lasting impression of our arrival in the canal was relief to the eyes; they could now rest on soft, leafy screens of poplars after the intense glare of the mirror-like river. One learns by hard experience simple things like how to pick a stop. The main thing is to avoid any lay-by or widening as these will be undredged and shallow. Similarly, the corners where the canal narrows into the jaws of the locks are always silted up. Apart from these it is generally safe to edge in slowly to the bank, boom out fore and aft with boathooks, and use the gangway to get ashore. Motor tyres are best for fenders. We carried six large ones and four small, which was only just enough, and also put a four-inch coir rope right around the hull. You must be prepared to go alongside either side and often there is no time to change. It is important to have some fenders slung low down because when the locks are full the stone work is scarcely six inches above the water.

On the second evening, Sunday, 3 July, June arrived, heralded by a thunderstorm. By now we were 53 kilometres on at Damazan. Sadly, Mike left us to fly home. We started late the next morning at 0930 to break June in gently and made a midday stop at Agen to find a bank, get tourist petrol cheques, and change to French bottled gas. In the evening we picked St Jean de Thumiac as a stop since it has an excellent Routiers Café and bathing in the Tarn close to the canal. For lunch the next day we chose Moissac in the basin, where there is plenty of water on the north side – just before it you meet two swing bridges which open at the toot of a horn.

Here the energetic Bruce Bolton left us. It was sad to see one of *Wild Goose's* best crews split up, but in the canal, as at sea, three is her ideal number and two are adequate. Our lock drill was now becoming more polished. It needs to be pre-arranged as giving instructions is difficult amid the roar of water at the gates. The shout of 'Lock in sight!' from whoever is steering, brings the crew from their sunbathing stations. June or I would steer in, fairly fast, as up to the watershed beyond Toulouse there is a current against you, coming out of each lock. You have also to be prepared to meet a strong crossing-stream coming out of the by-pass channel, pushing your bow over about a length short of the entrance. Then you come astern to check her and steer close to the low step located at one side of the lower gates for the *marin* (Alan in our case) to jump ashore and take the lines. I throw up our short stern rope, which Alan would make fast to keep us as far back in the lock as possible where the turbulence is less. June did the same with the head rope, which was led through a block on the bowsprit, and follows up on the winch as we rise. The water cascading over the upper gate is a cool, pleasant sight in the heat. Alan would close one lower gate, open a sluice, and I, in turn, would open an upper gate. Three cigarettes to the *éclusier* and off we went.

The next day we had only a railway for company, but we made good progress and reached Toulouse at 1700. Here you tie up in a great inland harbour. The centre arch leads on to the Midi. At that point, Alan, to our regret, had to take the night train for Paris. The following morning I was up at 0600 to buy petrol from an all-night garage beside the canal. It took two hours to negotiate four squalid city locks and we were held up waiting for barges. This involves delicate manoeuvring to avoid going aground in the approaches. You need to keep well back and avoid meeting the barge anywhere near the gates. The third lock, a double, lies under a road bridge. You hang on to the vertical bars recessed into the walls and begin to wonder if the water will stop rising before you are trapped.

The scenery grew even better. Green woodpeckers yaffled from tree-lined banks. The channel was narrow and winding between fields of maize and barley, but we were still going up and it was tough work as the locks after Bayard are oval and it was harder to avoid scraping. Nor was it easy to jump ashore. You had to clamber up off the mast.

Many of the bends are sharp, particularly where combined with a bridge, and there is always a risk of collision unless one is on the alert and uses the horn. Barge traffic is not so heavy in the Garonne, but beyond Toulouse it is in the order of 30 boats per week. Lock keepers can tell you if any barges (known as *peniches* or *chalons*) are expected in the next reach (*bief*). We made the top score of 21 locks that day and flopped into our bunks the minute the engine stopped at 2000 in a secluded *bief*. The engine made the cabin uncomfortably hot during the day and the relief from the noise in the stillness of the canal made the evening the best moment. The first hours in the cool of morning are also delightful. We managed a siesta most days between noon and three when the heat became almost unbearable. Amid the poplars and yellow cornfields we seemed at times to be sailing in a Van Gogh scene.

The next day we lunched at Castelnaudary where we had our only grounding in the dock short of the town. Misled by a moored barge, we picked the wrong side and came to a halt in glutinous mud. June promptly offered to swim across with the nylon to save launching the dinghy. By the time she had got to the shore, four Frenchmen helped pull her out. She proceeded to organise them into a tug-of-war team to pull *Wild Goose* off, so I hardly needed the winch.

At La Criminelle lock, June, after helping close the gates, was late jumping back on board as *Wild Goose* rapidly sank between the walls. I was concentrating on helping her down when we noticed that the tip of the mast which projected 12 feet astern was caught on top of the stone rim, so our stern was rising out of the water. There was already too much weight on it to push off with the boat hook. I shouted to the old woman in charge to shut the sluices; useless amid the roar of water and she was probably deaf anyway, but a single slash with the emergency knife cut the lashing. The mast leapt up and we slid away from the wall.

The next day we lunched at Carcassonne where the town is dominated by a fairy-tale fortress. It has been so restored that close up, it seems like a cardboard film set, but is splendid in the distance. We tied up that night for the third time alongside a familiar vessel, a big wooden barge called the *Joliot Curie* which we passed and re-passed daily. The next day we had arranged to meet Bernard at Homps. June felt poorly and had to endure the rigours of the fo'c's'le pipe cot while I proceeded through eight locks single-handed. Who can have said that 'he travels fastest who travels alone' – not a bargee.

At Jouarre Bridge the motor gave its only bit of trouble in the canal when the key of the water pump sprocket disintegrated. We had fitted a large filter on the water inlet for the voyage which had to be cleared a couple of times, and possibly the extra load while choked had caused trouble. Luckily, this happened within 100 yards of a good marine engineer and a new key was made. Just as the engineer finished, up drove Bernard by car: our first meeting since my wedding four years earlier.

We set off after lunch and made good progress to Homps. The basin here is another trap being very shallow, but the town, like Trèbes, is most convenient for shopping. Here Bernard recommended that we should turn south and come out at La Nouvelle instead of Sette as planned. This would save 50 kilometres and mean reaching the sea a day sooner which seemed welcome, particularly after his description of the mosquitoes in the coastal belt ahead. On the other hand, we had brought aerosol bombs and butter muslin to put over the hatches without so far seeing a mosquito, so were doubtful about this change. Several bargees assured us the route was deep enough, so we turned aside in the middle of the 35-mile *bief* between

Argen and Béziers and traversed half a dozen locks to reach the village of Salelles for the night. Salelles, with good shops and a small boat yard where barges are dry-docked, is small and secluded with tree-lined streets and has an air of mañana about it.

The next morning after the second lock, Moussoulens, we found we had to cross the Aude River, which would be difficult were it not for a large map painted on the arch of the preceding bridge. We lunched at Narbonne, which was a sea port in Roman times before the entrance silted up. At one point the canal passes by a tunnel right under a large block of buildings with poor sanitation. Fortunately, we emerged unsullied.

Beyond Narbonne the canal, although an adequate depth, became as narrow and reed-bound as an Irish sheugh, so passing or meeting barges was a problem. At one point we had to back half a mile to find a wide enough place to let someone past. For the last ten miles to the coast all one could see from the cockpit was mud and waving reeds. It was a thrill to smell the salt breeze, see the first gull, then get the first glimpse of the sea lagoons with small lateen-rigged fishermen at work.

We had taken ten days to get through. The weather that evening was unsettled and grey with rain and we wished we had stuck to the canal. But the next morning things looked up when a friendly Dutch schuyt agreed to step our masts. Even with the Dutchmen's help it took Bernard and me all day to prepare *Wild Goose* for the sea. The next day, Wednesday, 12 July, we reached Sette at 1830. With its picturesque port, Sette buzzed with life and glamour after a dull day of coasting on a lumpy sea in poor visibility and with a very light north wind. We were now overdue at Sanary, and June went on by train. Bernard rang the weather-man at Montpelier Airport. All I understood was the whistle the forecaster gave when we said we were going to sea. He spoke of strong north and northwest winds and a *coup de vent*, though he did not use the ominous word *mistral*.

We had little choice. Time was short and we were 100 miles from our destination. Even if there was a fair wind blowing offshore we had Bernard, a fine seaman. We took it like old gentlemen for as long as possible, keeping *Wild Goose* under-canvassed and running the engine at times when it seemed to assist the steering. The mizzen and staysail was the rig of choice at first; we were making five to six knots while rolling fiercely in steep curling seas, under a blue sky. 'The wind rises with the sun,' the fishermen had warned us and it reached its height about midday when we changed the staysail for the storm jib. It was mistral all right and dead astern, blowing the tops off the waves and throwing cascades of warm spray over the cockpit although the air was cold enough to make sweaters and oilskins welcome. Still, it was a phony blow to Northern eyes, for it had nothing like the power of a wind of equivalent speed at home. Even as we got farther offshore the waves grew no larger than eight to ten feet, and seemed much too small in comparison with the wind whistling past our ears. At 1500 the mizzen, the same old sail which split in three in Lough Swilly last year, developed a small tear, so I handed it and set the trysail loose-footed.

An hour later it seemed that we might reach Sanary in the dark. Alternatively, if we pressed on we just might make Cassis or La Ciotat in daylight, or again the wind might drop at sunset, so we decided to keep going. The sea was empty of traffic and a single trawler was all we saw the entire day. At dusk, a French naval aircraft approached from southeast, circled around us and withdrew; a comforting gesture but we were careful not to make signs that indicated needing help. An hour later it was obvious that the wind would not drop. It seemed to blow harder as the darkness increased. Heaving-to was an unattractive thought in this steep, uneven sea on a lee shore, so we altered course a couple of points southwards. Visibility remained good and we steered on the powerful light of the Porquerolles Islands and by dawn were close to Cap Cepet at the entrance to Toulon. The wind was beginning to drop at last, but it hardly seemed worth making full sail for the last mile and we beat slowly in under storm jib and trysail while I cleared one petrol stoppage after another. What a magnificent landfall it was; all the better after a rough night's sail!

In the morning sun a couple of gaily painted, local boats were hauling pots nearby and behind us dark green pines clothed the steep, red rocks of Cap Cepet which was surmounted by a gleaming white lighthouse. Beyond the calm, blue waters of the Rade the spires of Toulon floated in a smoky haze below the towering backcloth of stark mountains and reminiscent of Table Bay.

St Mandrier, a small horseshoe bay just inside the entrance, was our goal. Short of it lay the *Dixmude*, an aircraft carrier now in reserve, with a great spread of moorings fore and aft. The last petrol stoppage occurred just as we began to cross her bow. With our unhandy rig all we could do was bump clumsily down her side. We managed to hook up to a lighter at her stern, and during the ten minutes it took to clean the carburettor, the crew slowly awoke. They cursed us, sleepily, as they found their lines gone.

On Saturday, 15 July, we sailed *Wild Goose* back to Sanary. We arrived in the dark, but the next morning it seemed as if, after 1,200 hard miles, we had merely reached a place rather like Portrush: a horseshoe bay with a small artificial harbour on the left side as you approach, sheltered by a rocky headland with the town nestling behind it, a beach at the head of the bay and high ground to the right – but there the resemblance ends. Sanary is charming, full of life and colour, off the tourist track and drenched in sunshine. Bandol, where *Wild Goose* was to winter afloat, was five miles west of Sanary. We needed a mooring and a local man, suitably rewarded, to watch her. Bernard saw to all that with great efficiency. Then after a nerve-wracking drive to Toulon, he shovelled us on to the Paris train amid a pile of sail bags.

*****

Bernard adds:

Let me complete this tale with an extraordinary incident in Sanary. We sent for a mechanic who inspected Wild Goose's engine and said we would need to bring her closer into harbour. By this time Wallace had removed the accelerator and the clutch. He held the tiller while the mechanic was below, manipulating the engine as best he could. But communications failed. When Wallace said "slow down" the mechanic thought he should accelerate – with near-catastrophic results. To avoid a collision, I threw a rope onto the quay, yelling for somebody to tie it to a bollard. But there were no bollards, so somebody tied us to the base of a fountain. The boat came to a halt, but we were dragging the apparatus of the fountain, and a small geyser was now welling up instead of a stately gush. Wallace was happy that the boat was unscathed. But the harbour-master was not so amused. He used some French expletives to describe our unorthodox approach to stopping.

The following summer, Wild Goose was again in my care, after Wallace and his friends paid a short visit to Spain, but only reached the port of Rosas, a small, exposed place. I had to recover Wild Goose for a comfortable hibernation in France. This proved harder than expected. As luck would have it, I did not have the ship's papers which the Spanish harbour police wanted, so they denied me permission to leave port. So I took matters into my own hands. Just as night was falling, I boarded the boat after making the excuse that I had left some possessions in the cabin. The wind was blowing hard. A friend and I discreetly made all the necessary preparations for a quick getaway. In a matter of minutes, the boat was creeping rapidly along the jetty, as we cowered in the cockpit, sheltering from any stray bullets that the gun-toting Spanish police might fire at us. Remember this was the era of General Franco. In the darkness of night we passed Cap Cerbère and arrived at Port-Vendres where Wild Goose wintered happily.

CHAPTER 9
Sailing Through the Past
Two Triumphs of Reconstruction

Bruce:

In the summer of 1963, Wallace tackled the first of two great projects of maritime reconstruction which stand out as high points of his life. As well as bringing Wild Goose home from her Mediterranean adventures, he applied his gifts as a navigator and skipper to a far more public event: the recreation of Saint Columba's voyage from Derry to Iona, said to have taken place in the year 563. This voyage, in a curragh with 12 hardy oarsmen, was a major event in the life of the Anglican church and culminated in a grand reception on Iona, led by the Archbishop of Canterbury, Michael Ramsey. The journey had a strong religious dimension into which Wallace — whose character, people have noted, was always a mixture of earthiness and spirituality — entered fully. His partner in this project was the man who first thought of it: Canon John Barry, who at the time was rector of Hillsborough, south of Belfast. One outcome of the curragh voyage was to establish Wallace as an expert on early Irish boat-building and navigation. In this capacity, he was contacted 13 years later by Tim Severin, skipper of the Brendan, the 36-foot curragh that reached America's shores in 1977 and in which Wallace sailed as crew in the first leg, from Donegal to Iona.

The second reconstruction project took place nearly 30 years after the 1963 Iona journey, but it also involved a voyage from Ireland to Scotland. Wallace helped to build, and then skippered, a wooden galley of the kind that would have sailed those waters in medieval times. He thus helped to recreate the world of the Lordship of the Isles, a Gaelic-Nordic maritime kingdom that once held sway on the west coast of Scotland. His partner in this initiative was Ranald MacDonald, leader of the worldwide MacDonald clan. The voyage in the Aileach galley was more of a rollicking adventure and social event, though it clearly had its transcendental moments. When skippering an ancient boat sailing from Ireland to Scotland, Wallace seemed more himself than in any other of the roles he played in life. Wallace's obituary in the 'Glasgow Herald' was written by Maxwell McLeod, journalist son of the Reverend George McLeod who founded the Iona community and welcomed the curragh. Maxwell relished the fact that "by the time Aileach was launched, Wallace was (nearly) 65, yet he still slept on bare planks in the open air alongside his men."

Here is an extract from John Barry's book 'Joyful Pilgrimage' about the curragh voyage:

Sunday 9 June, Colonsay
We began the day, the Feast of Saint Columba, with Holy Communion. The life raft was our Holy Table and the sail supported by oars made an awning to give us shade from the early morning sun. Thirteen Irishmen on the sand of the Hebrides, with their curragh pulled up nearby on the lonely strand! This was a sublime moment of timelessness, when every circumstance of past and present merged and became one: the Gospel, the words of consecration, The Lord's Prayer, the place unchanged since the world began, and there were men of the Celtic Church seeking an island, going to Iona. Of all that we experienced on our unforgettable journey, nothing can have brought us closer to the very footprints of Columba and his friends.

On a slightly more down-to-earth note, Wallace wrote as follows about the challenges of reconstructing an ancient curragh:

Boats and sailing are mentioned more than 30 times in Adamnan's 7th century 'Life of St Columba'. There is ample internal evidence to show that the writer was familiar with sea voyaging and he made it clear that in St Columba's time passages between Iona and Ireland were made both in wooden boats and skinned covered curraghs. No details, however, have survived of the boat used on the original voyage from Derry, apart from the fact that she carried 13 men.

For the 1963 anniversary we decided to build a curragh rather than a planked boat for a number of reasons. The canvas covered curraghs now in use in the west of Ireland are direct descendants of the leather covered craft of the 7th century. In fact similar craft were observed by Julius Caesar when he invaded Britain in BC 54 – they were unlike anything he had met on the continent and the description included in his Commentaries is accurate of a present day curragh.

The seagoing Irish curragh can claim a unique system of construction and design almost unchanged for over 2,000 years. In fact its form is so simple and yet highly functional that it leaves little room for change. The primeval requirements of a craft which could be built without use of forge or sawmill and where timber is scarce, still remain in the west of Ireland today. Materials have changed certainly; tarred canvas has replaced greased hides within the last 100 years, iron fastenings appear in certain places instead of thongs, but despite such change of detail, the essentials of certain proportions for safe and effortless rowing, of a high bow for launching off a beach into the surf, and of lightness to allow for snatching her clear of the water and quickly to safety on men's shoulders have not altered.

Saint Columba, according to Saint Adamnan, sailed more often than he rowed. Present day Donegal curraghs sail not at all. Those in Aran and Dingle set only a tiny lug sail right in the bow for running and broad reaching, so modern practice gave no guide. Richard McCullagh (boat designer and first mate) selected a small edition of the Shetlands' sixarene rig – this is of Viking origins, possibly older; a local variant of the dipping lug and sets outside the shrouds. The sail made by McCready's of Belfast set beautifully, and in these calm waters we could make good a course eight points off the wind by pointing up five to six points off; leeway in even a moderate beam sea was of the order of three points. When we were reaching across to Islay from Portballintrae in Force 3-4, a fishing line trolled from amid ship made such an angle to windward that at first I thought it must have some sort of otter board on it, but it was just plain leeway! Apart from this the curragh stood up to her canvas remarkably well and ran 'like a sputnik.' The fact is that Richard designed and Jim Boyd built us a beautiful and shapely curragh, much bigger than any seen in living memory – a curragh of which we all became very proud and fond.

One of the high points of the galley voyage in 1991 was entering Fingal's Cave on Staffa – a place that Wallace first encountered during his early exploration of Iona and its environs:

I had cherished an ambition to take a boat into the cave for years and so I imagine had most of us on board. This was the chance of a lifetime. Within a few minutes we were manoeuvring so as to approach Fingal's directly from seaward, pointing *Aileach's* bows between its side walls of symmetrical basalt columns, twice the height of our mast. Overhanging the mouth is a jumble of broken rock reminiscent of a Grinling Gibbons carving. The champagne effect continues as you get close, borne on water so brilliant that it seems as if the white rocks below the surface are actually emitting light. Conditions for entry were pretty near perfect with enough movement of sea to make it reflect the dapples on the domed ceiling. We pushed our nose right into the entrance and kept a man looking out astern, as the swell was uneven and we had to be prepared to back water if a 'big one' should come up. Crewman Allan Turner led the chorus of a Gaelic boat song to produce harmonic and stirring echoes from the 60-foot high vaulted roof. This was by far the most impressive cave I have ever been into; the Blue Grotto in Capri is a mousehole by comparison.

Here is Wallace's overview of the Aileach's maiden voyage:

The idea of building a working replica of an Irish-Scots Galley started at a Clan Donald gathering in Skye in 1979. Ranald MacDonald and I first discussed the possibility while breakfasting on a sailing trip to meet some clansmen at Loch Boisdale. Around 3,000 galleys were built in the Isles in the 400 years after the end of the Viking era but not one has survived. That made it all the more of a challenge. As Captain of Clan Ranald, Ranald had access to many sources for information about design. Gradually we assembled the clues. These were mainly carvings on crosses and stones in Lorne and the Isles, and a few in Ireland. Mike Jarvis of Glasgow University helped to coordinate the material and supplied a lot more of his own.

Slowly the dream became a scheme. *Aileach*, meaning beautiful, was chosen as the name after a Scottish princess who in the 14th century married an Irishman – Prince of the House of Colla Uais, and hence a progenitor of Somerled and all the MacDonalds! It would become, therefore, a joint effort to celebrate the O'Malleys as lords of the Irish Isles and Grace's career in particular, as well as the MacDonald lords of the Scottish Isles. They all used similar galleys.

The galley was built in Moville, County Donegal, by James MacDonald & Sons below the Grianán of Aileach, where that lovely lady lived 1,500 years ago. Lofting started on the 1 January 1991, and over a month was spent constructing the laminated oak sterns and joining them to the one-piece keel. She was ready for sea by the end of April. Her hull was as lovely as the Princess herself; strong, light and perfectly shaped, with a bow like a swelling breast.

Flotation tests followed and we found her a delight to row, and for one afternoon in the sheltered Foyle she sailed fast and steered beautifully. There were no shortcuts taken with safety equipment. There was a tremendous send off from Westport by the biggest crowd of the whole voyage. The fair wind and bright sun gave a good chance to show off the linen sail emblazoned with the figure of Grace O'Malley, who we kept telling the Scotsmen was the equivalent of the Lords of the Isles.

We sailed to Clare Island the next day, from where Queen Grace ruled the western seas. We had a fair east wind and were well entertained when we got there. There was a football match against an island team. Their age ran from eight to late and as far as I can remember I saved a couple of goals, let in four and was told I'd done well for an oul' fella – I was 64. I think we must have won. I had to stand the drinks anyway.

The wind moved to the north. It was to stay there for most of the next six weeks. But luckily we didn't know that and were content enough with the current fine, sunny days. After rounding Achill Head we made Portmore for the night where it blew from the southeast. A bit of a dragging panic in the night ensued but all ended without bloodshed. After making two attempts from there to beat up inside Inishkea, the *Aileach* took the inshore route through the recently opened canal at Belmullet to Ballyglass, a useful small craft short cut. Then a calm though misty day enabled a close inspection of the Mayo cliffs from Kid Island to Pig Island, round Benwee and inside Boonbristy off Downpatrick Head. There a sudden breaker threatened to pour over the gunwhale but *Aileach*, after what an onlooker described as a 'tremendyus lep', rose and surmounted it and the two following ones in safety.

Overnight anchorages were found in the rock creek of Porturlin, and, for two nights due to bad weather, in the small artificial harbour at Kilcummin on Killala Bay. There some of the crew slept ashore in the newly decorated museum room depicting the landing of the French in 1796, but not before a couple of ceilidhs gave a chance for the Scotsmen to hear some Irish songs, sing some of their own and dance reels, while getting a fine flavour of Mayo company.

At Cooangar, a mile east of Easkey, the anchorage was a shallow gut open to the north between low slate on the west and a rough shingle shore. I'd never have gone in there without Irishman, carpenter and sailor, John Scott, as pilot. Anchored with 25mm nylon rope donated by Swan nets of Killybegs and a hungry crew ballasted with two fine salmon, we felt quite secure. The consistent headwinds had already put us way behind schedule so some hard rowing and a little time with the outboard got us 35 miles northeast, back on schedule and across Donegal Bay.

On 6 June the mast which had been bending alarmingly in strong winds a day before, broke quite suddenly in a 15-knot breeze off Portnoo. No one was hurt, as half expecting it, the crew had been sitting to windward at the time. In Burtonport two hours later it was shortened, glued scarfed, and finished by John Scott who helped in getting a pair of steel half laps made. This jury rig and some assistance from our dinghy enabled us to proceed the next day to Gola and Tory islands. The galley was then faced with the tough passage round Malin Head in strong north winds. After a two day hold up awaiting a favourable interlude at Fanny's Bay, it was a matter of getting round on Monday 10 June or letting down our sponsors further east. The mast could have gone at any time, so Deny Friel of Ballywhoriskey kindly sent two of his sons in their boat as escort. Some fifteen years before he had done the same for Tim Severin at the start of his Atlantic crossing in the *Brendan*, which I was fortunate to be onboard for a few days.

We got round the Head in fine style at six knots, surfing up to ten at times down the 12-foot swell. But there was no way I'd have risked it without help at hand, as we'd have been in trouble in such conditions if the patched up mast had gone. It had become apparent by this time that we could not move *Aileach* under oars in waves more than four feet high or against head winds of more than Force 4. Even light head winds made rowing at two knots very laborious. Ten oars had broken and some local curragh oars were obtained to make up numbers, but something better was needed. Our shore support party spent much time trying to find long seasoned blades but this proved surprisingly difficult.

Aileach would point up to about 60 degrees off the wind, but leeway, depending on the amount of sea, was from 10-20 degrees, so the net gain was small. Half a mile an hour actual gain to windward in Force 4 was about the best attained. Thus a five-mile passage could take ten hours! How did those ancient mariners manage? Fifteen miles a day was a big effort under oars. On each of the two days when the wind was fair we made around 50 miles with ease. *Aileach* would reach splendidly at five knots in a 15-knot wind and slip along at one or two knots in a scarcely perceptible breeze. Off the wind she was a joy to sail.

Next day, whistle stops at Portrush and Dunluce Castle where we entered a sea cave, once used as a galley port, in an unexpected calm after a blowy morning. After a three-hour pull we reached Rathlin, where they gave us a welcome which even by Rathlin's exalted standard was terrific.

On Wednesday 12 June, Cushendall, County Antrim, had planned a big evening pageant and celebration of the marriage in 1399 of one John Mhor MacDonald of the Isles to a local lass, Margery Bysset, heiress of the Glens

– a love match said the seanachaís, and property had nothing to do with it. So it had to be re-celebrated in style. By 1430 on the day it was blowing Force 9 and of course from the southwest, as we were now heading south! We were anchored four miles north of the pageant at the time, south of Torr Head, where there is an excellent anchorage close in on the north side which I didn't know about until Captain McNeill who runs the salmon fishery there showed me. There the ebb tide runs at nine knots – yes, nine! – close in off the point. We up-hooked an hour later and edged along the shore in a partial lee, then off Torcor the storm hit us. It was actually anemometered at Force 10 where it funnelled down the Glens. *Aileach*, with the outboard strapped alongside, just managed to fight her way foot by foot for an exposed mile into the river at Cushendun. There the pageant took place in spite of the horizontal rain. Admiral Sir Arthur Hezlet in his 30-foot Covic, *Agivey*, who had come round to keep an eye on us told me he had only once seen winds like it in his 40 years at sea. About as seasonable in June as a robin nesting at Christmas!

After two memorable days on Islay including a visit to the galley port at Dunnyvaig, the secret U-boat cove of Glas Uig, a tour of the distillery and various barbecues and ceilidhs, we made a slow passage to Oronsay in a cold, wet northerly – of course – and it took nearly three hours next day to beat round to Scalasaigs.

The weather turned up trumps, as it usually does for me, at Iona, which we attained after eight hours to windward, half oars, half sail. A day later we were able to row six miles to enter Fingal's Cave on Staffa for 'breakfeast' – this latter word came out as a misprint, but I thought I'd leave it, as all of cook Kevin's meals were feasts – perhaps the morning ones in bright sunshine best of all, with a huge boiling of porridge, endless rashers and mountains of scrambled egg, with toast, marmalade ad lib and excellent coffee. All the crew tip-toed forrard from thwart to thwart, or crawled if the tent was up, each clutching plate, mug and KFS. Then we crouched round the cook pots like the hungry savages which we'd in part become. A beat then to Ulva, past a small headland with a Gaelic name meaning point of a broken oar… we felt sympathetic for the person behind the name as we were down to nine oars now, including a bent one donated at Belmullet.

A lotus eating afternoon was then dreamed away all too soon in the peaceful non fish-farmed bay of Acarseid Mhor. Observing the north wind tending to fall each night, we next assayed a 16 mile tow round Ardnamurchan starting at 1900, well ahead of our fair tide. This was hard work but exciting and, with hindsight, one of the best experiences of the trip for me. The things which are hard to endure are pleasant to look back on, as Longinus remarked a few years back. He must have been a yachtie!

There was time to watch a glorious long, ever changing sunset melt into the afterglow and then become dawn. The black cliffs were close to starboard and each headland passed became a minor victory as we tried to find inshore eddies in our favour. Mark, our wise rowing master, relieved a pair of oars every ten minutes. This worked out that each individual rowed for half an hour, then had 20 to 30 minutes rest. It was a routine sustainable for many hours in that light weather, but frustrating and exhausting in a strong headwind.

By midnight we put Ardnamurchan astern, and feeling quite Homeric as the rosy fingered dawn appeared groped our way into the white sands of Canna. Ranald joined us there in his *Birlinn*, a Sigma 41. The boat would turn out to be most useful the next day. We had made it north against a north wind, now we tried everything to go east to Moidart in an easterly: endless tacking in mist and rain, then motor-sailing with four oars, then down sail and row. Finally, because we just had to, we pocketed our pride and got a short pluck from *Birlinn*. At last we made the south entrance, wet and weary at about 1600 and rowed the last mile in against a brutal ebb.

A big welcome and enormous tea greeted us on Shona which gave us the renewed strength to set up in the pouring rain a temporary roof over part of the original Banqueting Hall at Tioram Castle – a ruin since 1715 when it was burnt down, probably, it is said, to stop it falling into enemy hands. Sails and tarpaulins over oars kept the worst of it off and a huge bonfire dried the muddy floor. This was Clan Ranald's own party. Fourteen of his predecessors as Captains of the Clan had lived there. And what a night he made of it. Eating and drinking, reeling and singing until long after dawn.

On 30 June there was a formal welcome from three Highland Chiefs on Oronsay. After speeches came the Skye Pipe Band, dancing girls in the rain, and dinner in the dry. All thanks to Sir Iain Noble and his charming bride.

A day later, at dawn, the Shiants came into view as the wind failed. It took a four-hour pull to get the hook down off the low mole which joins the two main islands. The sea was studded with many varieties of seabirds. The picture made it clear why the Vikings used to refer to ships as the 'Ploughers of the Aukbirds meadow'. A day followed of guillemots soaring round cliffs, walks on high pastures, passages through tunnel caves and scrambles among kelp and boulders, one of the most bewitching I have ever spent in the Isles. The puffins flighted through the gap between the islands at a rate of 60 a minute, like the thickest packs of driven grouse you ever saw.

The evening found us beating once more. We finished just fetching Loch Brollhum on the Lewis mainland. It was to be our last night in the wilds and a bivouac for those who elected to sleep ashore. The chilly north wind proved strong enough to disperse the midges, and even the snores of the tented sleepers. After a virtually sleepless 48 hours, I, for one, really luxuriated in a peaceful night in the heather. It was bliss just to be able to stretch out straight and not have to try to kip curled between anchors, thwarts and food barrels.

CHAPTER 10
To and From Russia

Bruce:

The 1990s — and in some ways the remainder of Wallace's life — were a time of triumph and great adversity. Over the previous two decades, he and Wild Goose *had enjoyed lots of enjoyable touring in familiar sailing grounds such as Brittany or the Outer Hebrides. But from 1991, Wallace found himself negotiating much more testing seas. Months after completing the maiden voyage of his beloved highland galley, Wallace was helping to plan the most extraordinary trip that* Wild Goose *had ever made: a circumnavigation of Europe via the waterways of Russia, or to put it another way, a trip from the White Sea, in the Russian Arctic, to the Black Sea. Most of this voyage was successfully accomplished under the superbly competent leadership of his son Miles. It was a brilliant feat of organisation and seamanship, but one that left Miles physically and in every other way exhausted — a state of affairs which contributed to his premature death in April 1993, to the devastation of all his nearest and dearest. Despite the sorrowful aftermath, Wallace felt strongly that the Russia trip should have a place in his book of sailing memoirs. The best way to honour this wish, it seemed to the editors, was to record the parts of the journey in which Wallace participated: the first leg from Ireland to the Shetlands, and the final, triumphant section of the voyage through the Bosphorus to the Aegean which must rank as one of the happiest moments in Wallace's life.*

The fitting out of Wild Goose *for her Slavic adventure was a joint effort by Miles, Wallace and above all their cousin Stephen Clark. Stephen's gifts in all matters to do with engines were greatly appreciated by Wallace and Miles. Stephen then joined the first leg of the epic voyage, as far as Stornoway.*

This is how Wallace later recalled the conception of the Russian plan:

"What about sailing *Wild Goose* to Russia, Dad?" Miles asked the question as casually as he could across the round yellow breakfast table in the bow window of our Irish home. I almost choked on my porridge. It was October 1991. Miles and I had recently enjoyed a superb six weeks together rowing from Sligo to Stornoway as mate and skipper of a 16-oar Highland galley. I knew that Miles and his brother Bruce had been brainstorming some new challenge worthy of *Wild Goose* which had been our family yawl since 1956. It was a bright frosty autumn morning, the sort of day to make you long to be up and out on Hiawatha's 'shining big sea water'. Miles filled in a few details of the project as he saw it. Twenty minutes later over congealed bacon and eggs I was fully sold on the idea.

Nine months on, in May 1992, 'Wild Goose' set sail. This is what Stephen remembers of his 'Night Passage to Mingulay':

When it came to the selection, planning and execution of an expedition, Wallace was a 'one stop shop' in most matters. He had the background knowledge from his extensive readings, the network of friends and experts, that his personable skills could inspire and the sailing experience, honed from many a close call over the years, required to accomplish notable escapades. I was lucky enough to share in some of them!

When Miles announced his venture through Russia, Wallace's mettle was tested, and many people rallied around to assist in the unique voyage. Vast work had to be done from sorting the bureaucratic logistics and permissions for a private yacht to be licensed to traverse Russia, to the re-wiring and re-engineing of *Wild Goose* with her first diesel engine, updated communications, GPS (new technology at that time), along with a million other details.

The engine necessarily required three new fuel tanks, wiring, plumbing, gear linkages and a new exhaust system to be installed, by mechanics that could survive a breakdown by calling a breakdown truck, not see their lives in peril, engine-less, on a lee shore in a rising gale, with ice in the water. So it was that I found myself sailing as trouble shooter on the first leg of the trip, from Coleraine to Stornoway, because when I mentioned Wallace's abilities in most matters, they did not extend to engines, where a love/hate relationship existed. He loved to hate them, and treated them accordingly.

Wild Goose slipped her ropes at 0630 on a grey, drizzly morning with a rising southerly wind, and with a foreboding of 'what have we forgotten?' we motored north along the River Bann, each with a glass of Black Bush whiskey in our hands 'for the pier head'. A stop just inside the Barmouth for a couple of hours, to try to get some semblance of order into the ship, saw the old *Goose* rise to the first swell of the Atlantic shore shortly after midday. The course was due north, the landfall Barra Head on Mingulay, the ETA early morning the next day in Castlebay, Barra. The Malin forecast was southerly Force 6 increasing 7-8 later, visibility poor with rain. With jib and mizzen set and the engine driving at low revs *Wild Goose* swooped away north, her beautiful under-cut counter and canoe stern rising to the following seas. Unfortunately, with all the extra weight on board, the new heavier engine and fuel tanks, her counter didn't rise as high as it used to.

With so much equipment not yet properly stowed it was impossible to pass through the cabin to the fo'c'sle. There was gear everywhere, and as I turned in for a couple of hours sleep, fully dressed in oilskins, lifejacket and harness, I found I was sharing the port bunk with a 12-bore shotgun, an anchor and, perversely, a starboard navigation light.

I was woken from an uneasy sleep at 0200 by Wallace to take my watch. The mizzen sail had been handed, and with the wind now blowing a full Force 7 from the southwest, the engine and jib were power enough. "I think she's very low in the stern" said Wallace as he handed over the watch, "there seems to be an awful lot of water on deck." A quick check below showed that the bilge water was well above the cabin sole, but because I'd slept in my sailing boots, and climbed over the stacked gear, I hadn't noticed it!

Wallace started pumping with the big manual pump, whilst I burrowed through mountains of gear to reach the electric bilge pump and float switch only to find them blocked solid with sawdust and chippings from the re-fit. It was not an easy task in the pitch dark, arms underwater with gear falling about me, as we corkscrewed over the waves. The bilges were rather ominously filled with an emulsion of diesel oil, sawdust and water. The pump finally cleared, and the sea back where it belonged, Wallace got his head down for some sleep.

It wasn't to be for long. The wind was now rising to gale force, and we were flying along with just the jib set and the engine ticking over. I looked down into the cabin where father and son slept, exhaustion uniting them in their venture. The course was easy; keeping the wildly swaying mast just to the west of the Pole star, I was lost in the pleasure of helming, my legs braced across the cockpit, like a dinghy sailor, while we swept and swooped northward, the tiller alternately under my chin, or pushed away to hold her across the face of a wave, a big heavy old boat, acting like a confident soaring shearwater.

A nicely varnished piece of wood, about a metre long and heavy enough to hurt, landed in the cockpit beside me. I recognised it as a spreader that should have been ten metres up, staying the mast. "Need some help up here now," I shouted. Milo was up first, immediately realising that the mast was severely compromised. He was violently seasick over the side, before grabbing a hand-drill, nut and bolt, and insulating tape, and up the mast like a monkey, the wood in his teeth, he re-inserted it in its socket, drilled it, bolted it, re-led the cap shroud through the end of the spreader, before taping it in place. All the while, we flew north before the force of the gale.

Early morning spume saw us like spindrift, closing Barra Head. "See those two trawlers away to your west, they are likely to trip a wave, it will probably join you in the cockpit in about 20 minutes," Wallace warned. He was correct to within a couple of minutes, and the water gurgled, sucked out through the drains. By now the engine had died. Having run the first tank dry, we'd changed to the second, and despite being full the engine stopped. We then tried the GBD tank (Good British Diesel) that had been installed to be the 'all else fails' tank, kept full of clean fuel against poor quality fuel anticipated in Russia. The filler for this tank was out on deck and not properly sealed and with so much water on deck overnight, the tank was now about a quarter full of salt water, which the new engine had just ingested through all the filters, fuel pump, and injectors into its cylinders. We needed that engine to get us into the shelter of Castlebay, Barra, and Miles needed it to take him through Russia.

We spent 24 hours in Barra, moored just half a cable from a lee shore as the gale blew itself out. We removed the mizzen mast to reduce weight and left it on Barra. Miles re-stowed the boat while Wallace and I explored the pub. The following day we motored in flat calm all the way to Stornoway up the sea of the Hebrides past the west of Skye and the Shiant Islands, in glorious sunshine, while Wallace painted and Miles cleaned up behind him.

Bruce:

Flash forward now to September 1992... Under Miles's guidance, Wild Goose had successfully mastered the waters of the Russian Arctic — including an extraordinary stop at the Solovetsky archipelago, by turns a magnificent monastery (Russia's Iona, in a sense), and a terrible prison camp. One landfall was the little-visited island of Anzer, site of the Golgotha-Crucifixion church and a place where *countless prisoners were buried in a mass grave. (I revisited that terrible but holy place in 2001; by that time the church had been reconstructed and holiness was replacing horror.)* Wild Goose *had also negotiated the White Sea Canal, built by slave labour in Stalin's time, and visited such historic Russian cities as Kostroma, Kazan and Yaroslavl as she made her way down the Volga and then the Don. Like his father, Miles preferred the sea to any inland water, so there was a huge sense of accomplishment and of breathing more freely when, on 30 August* Wild Goose *left the Russian river system and emerged into the Azov Sea. Before negotiating the Black Sea, Miles said goodbye to the last of his excellent Russian sailing companions – who had included Nikolai, Vitaly, Galina and Arkady – and welcomed on board two experienced yachting friends from back home, plus… a few days later, his father Wallace.*

This is how one of Miles's crew, Lord Calum Graham, remembers meeting up with Miles and then Wallace:

After a night in Moscow, I took a perilous local flight to Anapa and taxi to Novorossiysk with Molly Ronan, the other crew member called up through Miles's network to replace Vitaly and Arkady, the two Russian crew members. They had sailed the Volga, Don and Azov Sea stages and were leaving *Wild Goose* in Novorossiysk. Bruce, conveniently posted to Moscow as a 'Times' correspondent, had played a big part in breaking local logistical log-jams in the organisation of Miles's circumnavigation of Europe and continued to do so in very kindly putting us up in his comfortable Moscow apartment.

Novorossiysk harbour, with its rusty freighters and the cement plant above it, looked grim but for the welcoming sight of the small, gleaming white, elegant lines of *Wild Goose*, the only yacht in the entire harbour, moored in an uncluttered corner. We didn't waste time in preparing for the Black Sea crossing, an eager Miles having already got cracking with most of the work before we arrived. With a reasonable weather forecast we slipped moorings on the 4 September and were clear of the harbour fairway buoy in short order.

We hove-to just outside Russian waters for a quick snorkel check of *Wild Goose's* rudder and propeller while Miles radioed to get through to Wallace and pass on a progress report. I could see this was a regular ritual. Wallace had been intimately involved in the preparations and working up of his dear *Wild Goose* and had lived and breathed the journey through Portishead Radio. We pressed on heading south by south west, close hauled on starboard for Inebolu on the Turkish coast with the wind picking up rapidly. The sea made it heavy going as we took in a reef in the night and banged into big breaking crests. When Wallace and Miles had fitted *Wild Goose* with a brand new engine, the extra weight in the stern meant something had to go to maintain weight balance and so the mizzen had been removed and Miles now could feel the affect of the resulting force imbalance on steerage. We made little more than two and a half knots, motoring to keep steerage in a lonely and very black sea.

The morning saw little progress and a lot of discomfort, with a unanimous decision to alter course for Sinop. In 15 seconds and 85 degrees of bearing off, our world changed to a sunny, dry, fast, rolling sail, damp kit out on the deck drying and Miles entertaining us enunciating his intended log entries in Shakespearian verse.

We had a warm, noisy and hospitable welcome from the trawler crew alongside whom we tied up in Sinop, followed by the opposite from the customs officer, furious that we had not moored off and waited for him and even more furious that the trawler crew were taking our side. Eventually ashore, first call was the hamam and a thorough steaming and brutal massage and a local lunch before victualling *Wild Goose*, Miles quickly tracking down a *dondurma* (ice-cream) to which he had been very partial through the trip. We made a bold but vain attempt to get a local meteorological forecast from the uncooperative NATO listening base on top of Boztepe Burnu, the hill above Sinop, returning to radio for a friendly and reliable picture from Bracknell.

The 8 of September saw us slip moorings early in the morning and head west along the Turkish coast, pounding close hauled again into a now veered west north westerly through the day and a tedious night. The early hours saw the promised further veer in the wind as we picked up speed and comfort, passing Inebolu and Kerembe Burnu in the morning, calling in at Gideros Cove on a superb afternoon. Miles had come in from a storm here in Tim Severin's *Argo* a couple of years earlier. With a swim ashore and fresh homegrown lunch we were ready to go again. We reached further west for an easy afternoon, gybing into Amazra in time for a harbourside dinner of fresh mackerel. The next morning we met a couple from the first yacht we had seen on the trip. Lee and Mel were two elderly 'live-aboarders' who had been on *Affaire de Coeur* for ten years and over tea on *Wild Goose* were keen to pass on the sights to see in Amazra that day.

That evening we slipped moorings and headed on westward in a bracing Force 4, reaching southwest directly for Rumeli Fener on the west side of the Bosphorous. *Wild Goose* rolled uncomfortably in the swell but at good speed, her auto-steering servo-motor buzzing this way and that as if she were muttering to herself as she picked her course through the swell. The lights of Zonguldac drifted past far off on our left as we lost sight of land and dawn on the 11 September brought us a sunny but cold day of seven knots sailing, a dolphin escort and a sudden increase in shipping as we approached the lanes at the head of the Bosphorous.

With raised trepidation over the task ahead in crossing the in and out shipping lanes in the night, we saw the lights of Rumeli Fener at 1030 and Miles called through Portishead to pass on our ETA to Wallace who was now in Istanbul. We weaved our way nervously past thundering live cattle freighters and container ships through the early hours and glided, relieved, into the small fishing port of Rumeli Fener before dawn, rafting up against big trawlers tied up four deep. Sleep was not an option as we then repeatedly slipped, moved and retied as trawlers one by one asked for room to manoeuver out of the tiny harbour through the breaking dawn. We were still rafted up against two trawlers at 1030 when Wallace arrived. There was a yell from ashore, the familiarity of which had Miles's beaming face with sun bleached hair pop up through the hatch and then the unforgettable sight of a clearly thrilled Wallace. He was scrambling over the thwarts and around the rigging of the two trawlers, waving aloft a bag of breakfast in one hand and a bottle of Bushmills in the other like a rodeo rider waving his hat. After a wonderful reunion, we sailed out of Rumeli Fener and headed south, as Wallace put it, "gaily daily sailing down the sunny Bosphorus."

Now let Wallace take up the story, starting at the moment of his joyful reunion with Miles:

W*ild Goose* looked a dream of gleaming blue water-line, white deck and hull with shining bright work unscarred by her far-sailing, the mainsail stowed for my inspection, her varnished mast gleaming in the morning sun and the Royal Cruising Club burgee fluttering on the masthead. I had never seen her look smarter.

The happiest of happy ships, *Wild Goose* slipped at 1030 to glide south before a fair north wind over a sparkling blue sea. The banks of the Bosphorus reached out to embrace us between soft green arms. There was a sense of awe at entering what is arguably the most historically important waterway in the world, and arguably the busiest. Its high sides are crammed with half-revealed beauty in many forms. Bell-mouthed at first it soon tautened into a channel about a mile wide. The shore lines were filled with interest: modern gun batteries mingle with forts and castles covering every epoch of the last 1,000 years. At Garipse, Buyuk Liman (a name that combines the Turkish for 'big' and the Greek for 'harbour') and later Buyukdere Cove, there appeared the masts of many yachts, ferries and coasters against a background of minarets, small houses and restaurants. Many of the latter had fronts of fretted woodwork so old that it had weathered to a dark chocolate brown. Some had windows a-tilt, adorning buildings that nestled at the foot of verdant green slopes hundreds of feet high. A flight of snipe-like birds skimming low over the water caught my eye: grey with a few speckles but showing no white as they twisted and turned in exact unison. There was nothing like them in my bird book. Were they the souls of Byzantine Christians killed at the time of the conquest by the Ottomans in 1453? No worry about masthead clearance as we passed under the two single-span bridges carrying road and rail traffic 100 feet over our head. Soon the ornate rectangular Ortakoy Mosque and the Dolmabahce Palace lay to starboard. Then we cut in east in a brief gap between crowded passenger boats serving the 16 ferry terminals. There were high-sided ferry terminals 'flying light' and unmanageable as their propellers thrashed on the surface. Ferry boats criss-crossing, yachts, deep-sea trawlers, rowing skiffs… At moments it was like the mad finale of a dream before waking. We were seldom on one course for more than a couple of minutes. But the local understanding of the rule of the road was good and I recall no near misses.

Next day, Molly Ronan and I braved the sea traffic again while Miles took photographs from the bridge of a hired motor cruiser. As we circled round, the main features of the city became familiar enough to have stuck in my mind ever since. On one side, the neglected waters of the Golden Horn; beside it the enchanting slim minarets of Hagia Sophia and the Blue Mosque. It was late afternoon as we came abreast them and made many passes for Milo to catch the pointed pillars against the setting sun as the waters of the Bosphorus turned from vermillion to purple. When Mehmet Batmanbek invited us to a Turkish dinner cooked by his stunning wife in the garden of his own marble-floored house overlooking the Princess Islands in the Sea of Marmara our cup of joy was full.

CHAPTER 11
Other People's Boats
To Greece (in 1972) and Far Beyond

Cleon, from the sprinkled isles that lily on lily overlace the sea
and laugh their pride when light waves lisp.
(Ancient Greek view of the Aegean)

Bruce:

Most of Wallace's seafaring exploits were in vessels on which he had placed his own stamp, either because he was the proprietor (Zamorin, Caru, Wild Goose) or because he was the first and most famous skipper (the curragh, the galley Aileach). As his yachting reputation, and business travels, ranged wider, he also had opportunities to sail in other people's boats' to locations he could never have reached under his own steam. Sales trips to the Antipodes introduced him to the bracing pleasures of sailing off Auckland and Sydney. With their friends John and Pat Fishbourne, Wallace and June also enjoyed sailing chartered boats in the Caribbean and the eastern Mediterranean.

The first reminiscence of a borrowed boat, in 1972, has resonance for me. I was almost 14. It was our second family holiday in Greece, and a chance to practise modern Greek, a language I love. As Wallace mentions, we visited Syros, home of the Greco-Irish Musgrave family who later became dear friends.

Wallace:

"Have you been out to the islands?" an elderly Greek inquired from the boat next door. We were in the process of backing *Winny* into her berth in the marina at Piraeus. "No," I responded wryly, "only to the outer harbour." Mike Villiers-Stuart had generously offered to lend us *Winny* for an Aegean holiday. The crew consisted of sons Bruce and Miles, my wife, June, my skipper-self, and Alan and Anne Parsons.

We duly arrived on Greek Easter Monday. Everything was closed. We could not buy bread, let alone find keys for *Winny* in the Marina Office. But she appeared in good shape, and once we secured access, it seemed we could sail the next morning. With the engine going, we set out to fill up with diesel. En route *Winny* started to go faster and faster, heading for an expensive motor yacht. Next a crunch, another two glancers and a bang brought us into the corner of a dock. *Winny* was unhurt, but a scar on the side of the *Pegasus* looked pricey. The owner proved sympathetic, and I settled up amicably.

Our first night out of Piraeus was spent at Poros. We berthed in the narrows that divide the island and the mainland: delightful and unspoiled. The next morning involved a 12-mile leg to Hydra, with a strong southeasterly. April is considered the start of the sailing season, a time with no marked wind pattern in the Aegean. The Meltemi that blows hard from the north only begins after June. So we were ready for anything.

We headed for Hydra, anxious to clear the Saronic Gulf and make for the Cyclades. It seemed obvious that a calm spell would last for 12 to 18 hours. The sea was flat, the sky overcast with no sign of wind and the glass steady. I felt tempted to head 50 miles east to Sifnos, but our crew had done little night sailing. Hydra, with its deep harbour, is a popular island, visited daily by steamers. Four attempts were required to get the anchor down, and to back into the right berth. The experts that already lay with sterns to the outer quay hardly hid their amusement. Picking the right place to drop the anchor and making sure it hits ground – whilst your stern stays pointing at your selected berth – is tricky. But we'd have hated to miss Hydra, where mules took us to the top of the island. In Greece as in Ireland, my weather sense proved sound. Even in faraway waters, the indications of sky, glass and 'feel' learnt at home proved more official advice. Following consultations with the weather service via the Greek Navy, and a promise of light conditions for at least 12 hours, we set off towards Kea, nearest of the outer islands. It blew like stink, but in the right direction. We had an exciting 50-mile run. At dusk we brushed a Greek steamer; then came the challenge of entering a scarcely lit harbour. It was worth the effort to wake up embayed in a new island. Unspoiled Kea has little connection with Athens. We found ourselves in a peaceful, wild bay with several inlets that reminded me of Ballynakil in Connemara.

Our next island, Syros, housed an Irish friend, Sir Richard Musgrave. We failed to make contact, though he was locally admired. A 'howdy' man on the quay gave a glowing reference, saying: "Good boy, Dick. Ireland boy, Dick. Always drinking whiskey!" Delos became the trip's highlight. It was once a holy island, also a centre of commerce, a slave market, and hub of the Cyclades. Hardly anyone is allowed to live there. Cruise ships make brief stops but we managed to stay overnight at Delos. We would walk the white marble streets, deserted except for lizards. The island's size, colour and atmosphere resemble Iona. We also visited smaller islets where on a grey day, seeing sandy beaches, stone walls, cabins and donkeys you felt close to Ireland.

Bruce adds:

*N*ow the camera rolls forward two decades. For our family in 1972, sailing in Greece seemed exotic: an opportunity that only luck and a kind friend could provide. By 1992, Wallace was more worldly, but sailing the southern tip of the New World still sounded like a remote, tantalising prospect. It was made possible through an old soul-mate, Euan Storey, who has roots in Latin America and Ulster.

Euan explains:

I began sailing with Wallace in 1952. I was 14 and Wallace was 26. But he never treated me as a brat; I always felt I was his equal. My summers were spent in Donegal, on a beautiful farm belonging to my Aunt and Uncle, Kath and Griff O'Donoghue. It overlooked the Swilly, between Malin and the Head. My first recollections were of sailing round from Portrush to the Swilly and crossing the bar in Caru, Wallace's first wooden sloop. We sailed Caru round the coast of Ireland, and once to the Isle of Man. We arrived at Douglas after a wet sail, looking shaggy. After getting Caru back in order we searched for a meal. We realised how we looked when every restaurant threw us out.

Years later my daughter Georgina was getting married and I invited Wallace and June. The idea was to combine the wedding with a sail round Cape Horn. A good friend, Curt Mundy, had his 38-foot ketch Ruby's Rascal down in Ushuaia, the southernmost port on Tierra del Fuego. Curt had sailed the oceans and was chartering his yacht to people wanting to visit Antarctica. Luckily Curt could fit us in for a week.

We arrived in Ushuaia and checked into a lovely hotel overlooking the bay. June graciously ducked out of our sail and spent the week with my niece. Wallace, Curt and I set off for Puerto Williams, the naval port of entry for Chile's south coast. Here we had to obtain permits to sail in Chilean waters, including Cape Horn. Once cleared, we set off on a beautiful evening and sat up most of the night enjoying the reflection of the stars in the black waters of the Beagle Channel. I was heading for my bunk when Wallace spotted what looked like a torpedo plowing through dark waters towards us. My imagination raced. Chile and Argentina were at odds over several islands and I had visions of us being mistaken for a stray Argentine ship. Luckily the 'missiles' we saw were dolphins, leaping into the air with sparkling effervescence cascading off their backs.

Next morning the weather was dull but the expected strong south westerly winds did not materialise and our sail to Horn Island was uneventful. Wallace and I wanted to land on the island and visit the Chilean outpost. Curt agreed to land us in the rubber dinghy and stand-off, awaiting our return as there was no ground secure enough to anchor Ruby. *We landed on a pebbly beach and walked up a track which zigzagged up the side of a cliff. We were greeted by three naval ratings; they would spend three lonely months before getting a break in Puerto Williams. The outpost consists of a small living area, a wooden chapel and a lighthouse. Our visit was an event for the keepers of this tiny realm! We signed the visitors book with entries going back a century.*

Back on board we lunched on fresh tuna with Chilean wine. We were sailing round Horn Island from west to east; in the distance we saw Skip Novak's yacht Pelagic *heading that way too. As we neared the impressive south side of the island with its 1,200-foot cliff and two horns sticking out of the grey seas, Skip came on the air to say his French charter party was preparing to swim off the Horn, possibly establishing a record. We three Anglophones agreed this was unacceptable to a boat flying the red ensign. Within minutes the three of us had stripped and were in the water. The sea was so cold that it did not take long for us to climb back on board, with French tourists busily photographing.*

By this time the wind was gusting up to 30 knots and it was time to be away. We sailed for the rest of the day without mishap and under short sail; we made excellent time with a following wind and tide. By night fall we were off Navarino Island which we had to leave to port to get back into the Beagle and make our way to Puerto Williams for more permits to sail into Chilean waters and the fjords. Curt went to his bunk at midnight; Wally and I stayed up yarning till I noticed the echo sounder reading very little water. I called Curt. We were navigating by compass as the night was dark and visibility was poor. I feared we were getting into shoaling waters. Curt had a look but returned to his bunk after pointing out that we were probably over a kelp bank. We kept going, reducing sail and watching the sounder. It was a daunting moment, stuck on a shoal bank near Cape Horn with a south westerly blowing up; we decided to play safe, drop sails and start the engine. Wally and I were creeping along when Ruby *touched bottom. Curt surfaced and we quickly reversed our direction. After checking maps and courses Curt realised we were sailing into a long narrow bay cutting into the middle of the island and had missed the west side of Navarino which should have remained to port. These waters demand luck and skill.*

We got back to Puerto Williams to find that our papers to visit the Chilean fjords had to be approved by Naval Headquarters in Santiago; this required at least 24 hours. So we invited the Commandant and his officers to a barbecue. After lamb, wine and whiskey, also enjoyed by other visiting crews, we convinced the authorities that our permits must surely include the fjords. Early next morning we set off for a wonderful trip up the Beagle to anchor in Garibaldi Bay. For three lovely days, we enjoyed incredible scenery, then sailed back to June in Ushuaia.

Wallace's account of the same trip:

"Swimming off Ushuaia's marvellous, Wally." That is what my friend Euan, who mostly lives in Hispanic places, said during his Irish trip. "Come next March. It might all be spoiled in a few years' time." I knew about Punta Arenas, the most southerly town in the world, and since reading Joshua Slocum had nurtured a longing to explore the Cape Horn Island. But I knew nothing of Ushuaia, or its role as a base for yachts.

I was soon to learn more. By March 1992, June and I were peering through an aeroplane window at mist swirling over forests on the snowy peaks of Tierra del Fuego, the Land of Fire. We descended through clear air to see the pale calm waters of the Beagle, a minute later we were taxi-ing along an airstrip on the water's edge. The strip stands where the Mission Station, the first building in Ushuaia, was erected 120 years ago. Of the Indians who lived there, fishing from beech-bark canoes, only a handful have survived. Today Ushuaia has hotels, ski-lifts, nature trails, even a night club. But it retains the air of a bustling frontier town.

Ruby's Rascal, a grey-hulled Nicholson 38-foot ketch, lay on a mooring. Alongside the finger pier off the Yacht Club we saw several other boats, some of them grand: Skip Novak's 56-foot *Pelagic*, three French yachts and a big American schooner. Next morning we cleared customs, a lengthy business since Chileans and Argentinians glare at each other suspiciously across the Channel.

A westerly wind gusting to 30 knots blew us swiftly between low shores, wooded except for a few clearings around scattered ranches. The beech forests below the snow-line were turning to autumn russet. Penguins dived at our approach, and a seal played around us like a dolphin. It is the warmest time of the year. "How is the tide running," I asked Curt, our relaxed American skipper. "Dunno… it doesn't make much difference around here." Curt is a laughing, informal sort of seafarer whose home is in Portland, Oregon. Stocky and straw-haired, he'd bought *Ruby* in Gibralter 18 years ago, kept her under the British flag and sailed her 100,000 miles.

We reached Puerto Williams at 1800 and tied up in a narrow creek. This is a hurricane hole as snug as any in the islands. If it wasn't for the jagged snow-caps of Las Dientes de Navarino in the background, and kelp geese grazing, you'd guess from the colouring and vegetation that it was Scotland. The wooden town is mostly naval and shops are limited. There is one small hotel and a restaurant; a ferry runs twice a week to Ushuaia. We meant to push on next morning as the weather was sunny and settled, but we were not allowed. It would take 24 hours, we were told, to obtain a cruising permit. This was a new form of control, and it involved getting clearance from Valparaiso.

Two days later on Saturday afternoon, the permit still hadn't materialised and only Euan's pleading with the signalman in fluent Spanish saved us from being held for a weekend. You can't dodge regulations here. A French yacht had been impounded and threatened with a crippling fine for landing clients on a prohibited glacier. Four Chilean torpedo boats stood ready to check incursions. HMS *Antrim*, renamed and under the Chilean flag, came in as we were passing east of the big island of Navarino at dusk. The Southern Cross hung brilliant above us. The star light in the clear air was bright enough to let us see our way between the dark silhouettes of Islas Picton and Nueva. It would have been hard to dodge kelp by eye but the main beds are shown clearly on the Chilean chart.

At about midnight I sighted what looked like a torpedo track coming at us. The projectile passed under our keel, turned and leaped across our bow, and then there was another. They were dolphins, robed in brilliant phosphorescence. A dozen gave a two-hour display of acrobatics. In pairs, trios and quartets of brilliant silver, they gambolled over a silken black sea, across our bow, a scene of beauty no theatre could match. I came off watch regretfully at 0400. The ship's cat, Jizzy, settled on my tummy just as Pwe, a Siamese belonging to my friends the Smeetons, used to when we were sailing their boat *Tzu Hang*.

At dawn our bows were nosing into the Sound between Wollaston and Deceit Islands. We plugged through small tide rips into a biting Force 4 westerly, past Puerto Martial on Herschel Island, the only permitted anchorage in the group, and by 1100 turned south for the Horn itself. Hall Island, humped like Ailsa Craig, was the next mark. Then jagged rocks known as the Cathedral came into sight at the NW corner of Horn Island. Historians say the Cape is named after Hoorn in Holland, but those twin spikes must also have inspired Lemaire, who christened the Horn.

Cape Horn Island is a wedge; it rises 1,200 feet and is about five miles long by about two wide. The impression is of a reduced version of Scotland's Barra Head. There is a surprising amount of vegetation on the south and east sides. Only the west, where the greybeards run 70 feet up the cliff in gales, is bare. But nourishment for animals is scarce. It seemed almost dream-like, to be looking at this cape of ill fame in calm conditions, with a two-foot swell and moderate fair wind under a lightly overcast sky. The event became real when Curt celebrated our transit of the head by opening champagne. Then Euan peeled off and jumped overboard. Perhaps he was impressing the French clients on *Pelagic*, a cruising yacht to seaward. The girls looked away of course as Curt and I followed, but there wasn't much to see as we emerged after a few dozen frozen strokes. The sea was about as cold as Scotland in April, but more phosphorescent and salty. My brother Henry later dubbed me the first Irishman to swim round Cape Horn.

We anchored half an hour later in the midst of thick kelp on the east side, and puffed our way up wooden steps to reach a boarded path over a bog to a radio hut. The station is manned by three Chilean naval ratings. They appreciated a gift of magazines and food, and gave us coffee. We were shown the light, a capella or chapel built from logs with room for about a dozen people, and a memorial plinth dedicated to Cape Horners of old who did it the hard way.

Our next objective was the *senos* (fjords) or glaciers 50 miles west of Ushuaia. Sadly the shortest way to them, east of Navarino by the Murray Channel, is *prohibada*, so overnight we retraced our outward passage. It was now gusting up to 30 knots astern, but *Ruby* kept us safe and dry. A second stop at Puerto Williams was necessary to check out of Chilean territory and into Argentina. There was a splendid *pasado* (barbecue) where Euan roasted a sheep. It was attended by crews from half a dozen yachts, among them Nick Pyle from Seattle. I told him I didn't feel like a Cape Horner. "I do," he replied. He'd driven his big schooner all the way from home, and endured a dirty night at Puerto Martial in 70-knot conditions.

A day later we were motoring *Ruby* windward in milky water between 1,000-foot tree-clad cliffs as we approached the Garibaldi Glacier. Our chart was a Xerox of a small-scale Admiralty one, and some channels had their ends marked, intriguingly, by dotted lines and the word 'unexamined'. We also had a hand-drawn plan of the glacier approaches.

These aids sufficed, for most of the coasts are clean, but you need a good lookout, no chart can locate floating ice.

The glaciers were, for me, a very new experience. I'd never picked a route through small floes, tight enough packed to look a solid mass from a distance, but opening into channels when you got close. I had never hove-to just one cable's distance from a glacier emitting rumbles, bellows and reports. Every few minutes vast lumps of ice fell down 100-foot crystal cliffs to create splashes and set *Ruby* a-dancing. The sun came out at intervals to backlight the scene and show off the translucent electric blue of old ice in fissures. The floes shone in curious, inspiring forms. One piece, resembling a frog on its back, nudged aside a caravel in full sail, only to dodge a crocodile with jaws ready to snap two love-birds emerging from the next floe... new fantasies every minute. An unforgettable trip!

Bruce adds:

As a final sample of Wallace's adventures on other people's yachts, here are notes he made from a partial Atlantic crossing with his Royal Cruising Club friend John Hodges, a Yorkshireman whose land-life – like Wallace's – involved producing textiles.

John writes:

We were on our way back from the Caribbean in our Rustler 36, Artemis. Wallace joined us in the Azores and we had a smooth passage to Wexford. For the first week we motored in a flat calm; then the wind filled our sails and we approached Ireland in a near gale, the roughest weather we'd encountered on our Atlantic circuit.

The crew was my wife Pauline and myself, plus a great sailing friend, Guy Rooker, and Wallace. We loved Wallace's rich fund of stories. Guy, a doctor, watched discreetly as Wallace coped manfully with his diabetes, a condition he developed recently. After a tot of Jameson's whiskey, he would plunge a syringe through his red canvas trousers. The regime seemed to work. Wallace wrote copious notes, I am pleased to see them reproduced here. To quote one of his own favourite expressions, he was a great shipmate!

Day three: No ships, almost no wind, and no dolphins. Dolphins seem to come in the evening. We saw bottlenoses playing around the ship at least four times. A turtle, 18-inches long, with the top of his shell clean and polished, but underneath covered in mussels, was probably ill.

Lots of deep blue By-the-Wind Sailor jellyfish; flocks of 40-50 of them passing all the time, many of them very white, presumably full of eggs. Less shearwaters – probably only one or two all day as we were getting out of the range of where they nest on the Azores. Swell more oceanic, longer, and now much more on the beam with a height of about six foot. A lovely slice of palest blue sky to the east.

No stars tonight or last, just a glimpse of the half moon at midnight and some moonlight shining through the cloud and making a silver patch on the water far astern.

Day four: Thursday night, midnight. The wind came at last at about 1630 this afternoon. We had sailed at 1400 on Monday, motored all that day, Tuesday and Wednesday, and now out of the Azores' high in the Charcot sea area. My watch is 2300 until 0200. Guy follows, then John. Now the west wind fills the Genoa and the main is broad out on the beam – we're pushing through the custard, as an Australian put it, at five to six knots in a series of rustly surges. The sea is jumpy and uneven. *Wild Goose* would have been less jumpy. Saw our first ship today, four miles off – a blue hulled container ship bound for South America. Guy gaffed a big grey fish, after it and others refused to take the bait. We tied a big fish hook to a broom handle and he gaffed it in the gills – a sea bream or porgie, about four pounds, which Pauline put in an excellent pie.

Saw shearwaters of the southern type several times, keeping very shy of the ship, also one dark petrel, like a 'stormy', but bigger and black. Shearwaters come up much closer at night, they appear to circle round *Artemis* at dusk. We are further north and it is colder. I don oilskin trousers, shoes and a woolly hat on watch. But in the afternoon we had perfect sun bathing conditions – the sea was a Mediterranean blue, the breeze gentle. The swell was smooth but many faceted and five-foot high on beam.

Day six: Gusts and squalls from the west – double reefed, single reefed, double reefed again. I learned how to single line reef from the cockpit and tauten the canvas spray hood. Re-reading Slocum's book about sailing round the world, full of humour and originality. His first adventure with the *Pinta* was on a passage from the Canaries, so in these waters.

There are still many sailing jellyfish around us, bigger and bolder than the ones we saw in the Med. The sail is set across its body at about 45 degrees like a mainsail for reaching and there is a ridge of dark blue along the top in a pretty arch.

Day nine: Exhilarating sail! Double reefed main and blade, forceful seas – some roaring down and bursting just to weather of us, like a great whale breaching. The wave-tops look like the heads of horses with white manes streaking down their backs, particularly on a wave pinnacle like a campanile, to mix the metaphor. There is a great bridal train of white water alongside on the quarter looking open and filmy and gleaming in the sun, and continuously being renewed as we forge ahead. I admired the magical efficiency of the self-steering gear. What millions of hours this could have saved over the centuries. Blondie Hasler was the inventor. It is strong, efficient and silent.

Day ten: Excited about approaching land. By morning we were only 40 miles off the coast and had one of the finest exhibitions of bird flying that I have ever seen – birdobatics! The stronger the wind the better the shearwaters can fly. They appear to dip a wing-tip in a wave top before tilting up into the sky.

CHAPTER 12
A Stormy Brush with History

Bruce:

Wallace became intrigued by a yachtsman who sailed the Celtic waters two centuries ago. So in early 2009 he made a plea for information about Robert Harvey and his travels on Rambler, a 30-ton sloop. Here Wallace introduces excerpts from Rambler's log of a trip from Trawbreaga Bay, Donegal to Scotland in 1814. He then describes his re-enactment of the trip, in summer 2009, which took a dramatic turn. This account is rear-guarded by helmsman Graham Kane, with a fine observation from Ros Harvey.

Wallace writes:

On 20 July, 1814, my kinsman Robert Harvey of Malin Hall, left Trawbreaga Bay in Rambler to cruise the Western Isles. Yacht cruising was then almost unknown in the north of Ireland. On the dining room table of Goorey Lodge, Malin, where Robert Harvey's portrait casts a roguish eye, are marks made by his nephew Gardiner Harvey when he danced on it as a boy to celebrate Waterloo. That was soon after Rambler's cruise.

There must have been many heel marks on the cabin sole of the Rambler too, for Robert and his cousins, Robin and Ralph Young, danced, sang, flirted and wined with an exuberance many a modern sailor would envy. Robert's descriptions of scenery and his enjoyment of pipes and reels, punch and porter, makes one realise what fun they had. The rest of Rambler's company consisted of Skipper Jack from a Glengad seafaring family, Ned as Cook and Gilbert Brown, probably from the famous wildfowling family of Inch Island, Lough Swilly, as Mate and Bagpiper. Along with them was Robert Harvey Junior aged seven. A big adventure for him! He later became a country parson and seems to have made no other cruises.

Excerpts from Rambler's log – as copied from Robert Harvey's notebook (Spellings and syntax as in the original; Wallace's text in parentheses):

20 July: Left Strawbreagy with wind at southwest, had a severe touch on the bar, but did not make any water by it. Cleared Malin Head at about noon, and steered a nor-east course all day with a fine breeze for Isle of Mull. Ralph and Robert both a little sick.

Early 21: Saw land to the eastern. Steered for it, thinking we were up with Mull. Round a headland, and ran up inside. Ralph and Robert better, ate breakfast, having spewed a litter of pups all night. Went on shore, found ourselves in Colonsa (Colonsay). ... Sailed again nor-east, and made Mull in a thick fog and rain. Not sure of the land, but hail'd a fishing boat that told us. Night coming on but they would not give a pilot under a pound. Gave them a dram, and tune on the pipes and dismissed them.

22 July: At 9 this morning sailed with a light breeze that only just brought us out of the Lough. We were then quite becalmed, and only just doubled Ruinafin (the east point of Loch Spelve), intending to run round Mull by easter'd to Staffa, but logg'd without wind until 5 on Monday.

24 July: I don't think we are ever doomed to see Staffa, for this morning at 9 o'clock we left Tobermory, and two other pleasure boats along with us. We pegged on all round Mull, and put in here, Camsallagh Bay (Loch Cuan) for the night. We then got our fire lighted up, but the mutton chops that Ned got ready seemed too few for three hungry fellows, so I took the knife, and Robin the hatchet, and if we are not full enough of chops just now, the devil's a witch. A boat crew have just come on board. They can't speak anything but what I can just follow in very broad Erse. We have asked them for eggs, as ours are finished, and they have only promised they will bring us 'hags' in the morning, but whether they may be fresh enough for our delicate stomachs, time will tell.

26 July: Tuesday morning, 7 o'clock. Devil a bit nearer Staffa than ever, nor any attempt to be made today at all. However, we shall have something pleasant substituted in place of it. I have gone on shore and am just returning with a famous Scotch piper playing in the little boat. We have taken our tents on shore, and will dine there. ... We have just returned from Mr Campbell's at Tirsanish (Treshnish, near Ensay the southwest point of Mull) where we spent a very pleasant evening, some reels danced to the Scotch pipes, and very civilly treated. On coming away we got a great quantity of fresh butter, fine milk, and a quarter of the very nicest small fat mutton. Young Robert has got hold of a letter from Miss Kitty Campbell, which she covered the butter porringer with; if it is as pleasant to him as her lips were when we were coming away, it must be pretty comfortable. He kissed the whole family, and only for his father and Ralph would have, right or wrong, brought one of the girls to Malin in the *Rambler*.

28 July: About three o'clock we really did reach Staffa, and went on shore, and then rowed round it in the little boat. Entered Fingal's cave, the most wonderful, the most awful, the most tremendous and the most extraordinary natural curiosity I ever saw, well worth all the loss of time we underwent to accomplish it. I stayed for an hour on the island and shot a seapye (oyster catcher). From thence we got a fine breeze and sail'd for the Island of St. Columkil (now Iona), beside which we arrived after dark, and are at anchor just off where the Kings were buried.

29 July: This morning was calm. We saw the ruins of the famous old church, beside which so many royalties were buried. The man who attended us said there were 28 Scotch Kings, eight Norwegian, four Irish and one French buried there. ... About four o'clock in the evening we set sail to get out of the harbour, but with adverse wind steered for Mull. Then a jybe broke the gaff. We were very much in the dark, so we were obliged to stay out to sea, and after a very squally and severe night, we anchored on our old ground off St Columkil, where we have remained the whole of this day in consequence of the squally weather and getting our sails and masts repaired. Jack could not get any tobacco for his Irish money, so you may guess in what humour he is in.

2 August: Reached Oban... a very cheerful and pretty regular built town, all the houses two stories high, very civil and industrious people. We have purchased gunpowder, rope, porter, sealing-wax, comfits, blacking liquid, gloves, turf and bread besides many other small eatable matters, such as mutton and potatoes, also pen-knives. Even Robert got a new westc't and trousers made. This is a great fishing place and there were some herring taken last night, but before we could get any of them they were all salted.

4 August: We set sail about eight o'clock in company with two other sloops, and the *Rambler* with her gaff topsail drawing well beat them every one hollow and brought to in this harbour, Easdale, famous for a remarkable slate quary, about five in the evening. The evening continues very severe and incessant rain, not withstanding which we have been very cheerful and lively, and I must say that Robert is no small addition to the party. Though confined to a narrow Mess-room we are not without our comforts, songs, punch, porter and bagpipes, and many jokes from old Jack and Gilbert, and common eating of mutton chops, and new potatoes. I think we all look forward with pleasure, however, to our old land. Wind and weather permitting, we hope to see it very soon, but nothing is certain

for us sailors. So we never frets about trifles. The two sloops that were behind us are just arrived here after drudging at sea three hours against the tide and their sails reefed one half at least. So much for beating to windward in style.

9 August, Sunday morning: About 9 o'clock we set sail for Ireland from Jura in a favourable gale, and got along Isla almost to the most southerly point, but the wind became quite slack, and changed to the southeast, so that having no hope of reaching any part of the northern coast, we thought it better to put into this harbour, Loughdomish (now Port Ellen), where we found four sloops – one bound for Derry, and three laden with stone, bound for the Batteries in Lough Swilly. We are all waiting for a northerly blast, which we hope soon to get. Ralph went on shore after dinner and walked a mile on the road towards Bowmore, where there is a Custom House. And great trade it is. We met with Dan'l Bane from Rathlin here, and we were on board his sloop. We may regret our delay, but there are twenty sail before and behind us, all in as anxious awaiting as we are. Ralph shot two puffins in the Sound this day; could not get a shot at a gannet since we left home, though we saw many of them.

12 August: Our third day in this island and a more dreary, wet, stormy looking one we have not had since we got to Scotland. I have just been advising Robin to go on shore and endeavour to get a beef cow to buy, for there seems to be no chance of our getting home till this summer weather goes away – and possibly the winter may bring us a north or east wind which is all we look for. Even the packet from Greenock to Loughindall could not reach the latter place in the gale, and put in here a little after us, full of passengers to go overland to Bowmore. Jack has taken the men on shore and Robin has given him a guinea note, and I understand as long as that lasts, we need not expect to see any of the party.

15 August: We set sail with a northwest wind for Mallin; but when we got to the headland of Isla we saw it was impossible to make the coast of Ireland, and so determined upon coming to the harbour of Cambelltown. It is now nine o'clock and we shan't go on shore till morning. Dan'l McCuigan went to Rathlin and took our letter this morning, so I hope we shall be heard of soon, if not seen.

*****

Wallace on the first leg of the *Brendan* voyage, 1976
(Wallace Clark Collection)

Wallace and crew under oar in *Aileach*, 1991
(Miles Clark Collection)

Lord of the Isles:
Wallace on *Aileach*'s
prow, 1991
(Wallace Clark Collection)

Aileach at the cave
beneath Dunluce Castle,
Co Antrim, 1991
(Miles Clark Collection)

Wild Goose off a kremlin, Solovetsky Islands, Russia, 1992
(Miles Clark Collection)

Wild Goose on the Bosphorus, Istanbul, 1992
(Miles Clark Collection)

Sunset off Hagia Sophia, Istanbul, 1992
(Miles Clark Collection)

Sunk in sight of home: *Wild Goose* at the Barmouth, River Bann, 1998
(Kelly Allen Collection)

Miles and Wallace
(Tony Traill Collection)

Bruce
(Sarah Clark Collection)

Wallace with his grandchildren
Finn and Georgie
(Wallace Clark Collection)

June and Wallace, circa 1990
(Bruce Clark Collection)

Croatia, 2010: still at the helm at 83!
(Des Moran Collection)

Wallace:

Here the log ends except for a scribble about a call at Rathlin. In the hurly-burly of a hasty return, it can be an insuperable effort to record the last day's sailing. We may imagine them making a fast passage home in the lee of Irish cliffs. Perhaps they called for the sake of a tide at Rathlin, where Robert's in-laws were the Gage lairds. Shopkeepers in Iona would still look askance at Irish money. I doubt if many modern yachtsmen could solve a shortage of mutton as effectively as the *Rambler's* crew. French fishermen still, I suppose, poach sheep on islands but no longer risk hanging. Today's yachtsmen wouldn't shoot puffins and gannets, we may gain a point there, but you would look a long time in Port Ellen now to see 'twenty sail' awaiting a fair wind to Ireland. Nor could you send a letter direct to Rathlin. We have lost the old cross-channel boat traffic, and the ties of family and friendship between Ireland and the islands. Fifty years ago an old Portnahaven man told me: "Half of Islay used to go to the Old Lammas Fair in Ballycastle, and Donegal horses would have filled the streets at the fair in Bowmore."

In 2009, in my effort to repeat the voyage of Robert Harvey, I was joined on *Agivey* by Ros Harvey (a descendant of Robert) plus Graham Kane and his son-in-law, Ashley Nagle. The first leg was planned to take us from Malin Head 30 miles north to Portnahaven. It began as a dull passage, with a fitful wind, low visibility and a low silver-grey swell rolling in from the west. Not a vessel in sight. In Harvey's day, there would have been open boats fishing with lines, brigs and schooners on coastal passage, or smuggling cutters running inshore to land French brandy or American 'baccy' on Inishowen. We had lost sight of Ireland by 1300. The Area Shipping Forecast at 0520 had been favourable. Graham's visit to the Malin Radio Station had indicated nothing more than Force 6 to follow.

It was 1730 before we got our landfall – a dim glimpse of Orsay Island. What looked like flashes of white indicated breakers along the shore, nothing unexpected. We'd planned to be entering at 1830 when the tide should be slack. A convivial send-off at Portmore, Malin, delayed us one hour, so now we would be arriving as the tidal stream started to run east to fill up the Irish Sea. But this should not yet be at its full strength, which in mid-tide reaches eight knots.

Our friend Des Moran in his boat *Nanette* was a couple of miles ahead. The swell was now running nine-feet high and becoming shorter. Confident in Graham on the wheel, I went below to make tea and have a rest. Then Graham called up: "Better come up, Wallace. A lot of white water around." With barely a warning, we were surrounded by a patternless array of green-faced pinnacle waves, cresting into white finials above our heads. We appeared to be in the midst of ten-foot high white horses, forming a circle of say 30 feet in diameter. A term used rarely on Admiralty charts describes what we saw: 'great overfalls' – defined as waves 'caused by a strong tidal current setting over a submarine ridge or shoal.'

The sea around us was a continuum of white peaks with deep hollows between. Graham eased engine speed to 800 RPM, enough for minimum steerage-way while keeping the sails full. *Agivey* began a series of mad corkscrews, putting her bows-down green wave faces that seemed almost perpendicular, and rolling to port or starboard before rising to point her full length at the sky. We were indeed entering just what I had planned to avoid; the tide race of An Coire – The Cauldron. *Agivey's* high flared bow and three-foot topsides, giving much reserve buoyancy, stopped us taking heavy water on deck. But for how long? The tidal stream might increase in strength during the next hour. If we shipped a big green one or two into the cockpit, it might be hard to keep afloat. I started the electric bilge pumps aft of the engine and under the main cabin, just in case. Life jackets would be of limited help. The jabble around us could have dashed suffocating spray into a swimmer's face.

While Graham fought *Agivey* along, I searched for a way to less dangerous water. Breakers I had seen on previous visits were smaller and closer to Orsay. I have a mental picture of the full length of the inside of the twelve-foot *Blue Boat* tender which we were towing – making a 90 degree nose-dive down the face of a wave close astern. Moments later both short painters snapped and she disappeared. A relief – if she had crashed into us, damage could have resulted. Ros glimpsed the *Blue Boat* perched on a wave top before sliding into the next deep sea hole astern. Then I worried how the diesel feed to the engine could survive such antics in every vertical and horizontal plane. But the good old BMC engine, fed by the new stainless steel tank, never missed a beat!

Graham kept our head facing north west so far as possible to stem the tide, while taking each opportunity of edging east towards the land. Without this sideways movement we could be trapped in the maelstrom for hours. The atmosphere was tense as *Agivey* gallantly rode over wave after wave, out of one abyss and into another. For a full half hour we seemed to maintain our bearing on the white lighthouse tower on Orsay.

I have often been in tide rips: frequently in the Corryvreckan between Jura and Scarba; twice in the Grey Dogs two miles further north; many times in the 'Seven Tides' of Rathlin Sound; occasionally in 'The Merry Men of Mey' off Orkney; and in the fierce six-knot ebb out of Strangford Lough and the Raz de Sein in Brittany – but never experienced anything nearly as bad as this. It is curious how often the nodal point of a tide can have a local effect of killing the breeze. It did so now, I was thankful. If any gusts had blown up strong enough to make the wave tops break above our heads, we'd have been scuppered. Thankfully we edged across to the south point of Orsay Island before dodging east of it to the Channel inside. It was a slow going up the sound against the tide. A welcome sight was *Nanette* at anchor off the village. Soon we were circling her; Des said they'd also had a bad time, but no damage.

I picked up the vacant mooring which we had been allowed to use two years earlier. Portnahaven fishermen were, as usual, most helpful. Beside us was a cheerful looking angling boat called *Free Spirit* and a big red motor fishing vessel named *Colon More*. Poole, painted below as her port of registry, was a reassuring name. I had got to know all Poole's islets when minesweeping in 1945. Her skipper Ken Woodrow gave helpful advice: "Weather's broken for a couple of days. You'll be snug here in the meantime. That rip tide? Caused by a 1,000 foot underwater cliff, stretching seven miles out beyond the islands." I realised that anyone fishing out of this harbour must be brave and clever. We yachties don't bother much about deep soundings, but now, looking at the chart, I could see how the depth increases east of the 20 fathom line south southwest of Orsay to 50 fathoms within a quarter of a mile east.

On Thursday, good as his word, Ken warmed his engine soon after 0600. He called to see if we were ready. I've never dared to use the northern exit which looks so rock-strewn, but he made it simple. He took us very close along the Islay shore until we reached a curved, pebbly beach a little past the north end of Muilleach Island. Then he headed west, leaving the ominously named Rudha na Faing well to starboard and two small above-rocks north of Muilleach close to port. A farewell wave and *Colon More* disappeared.

Graham writes:

The usual early year missive arrived from Wallace. A barely legible note suggested a trip in the Agivey to the Scottish Isles, tracing the route of Robert Harvey. My imagination was fired by the Rambler crew. I was pressed into going. I also suggested that my son-in-law, Ashley, a sporty, fit type, join us as young muscle. Wallace jumped at that, and so the crew were organised: Wallace the skipper; Ros Harvey, a descendant of Robert Harvey, as artist in residence; Ashley for youth and strength; myself the cook and helmsman. Our friend Des Moran offered to bring his yacht, Nanette.

On a damp Monday morning recalling John Masefield's 'grey mist on the seas face and a grey dawn breaking,' well-wishers congregated on Portmore Pier for an auspicious send off. The craic was mighty and longer than planned; we left Portmore over an hour behind schedule. Wallace was tempted to go into Inistrahull to overnight but decided to proceed to Portnahaven on Islay. The wind and tides were with us so we made good progress. Nanette forged ahead as we got into sight of our destination and Wallace decided it was time for a zizz. I was at the helm when, in my peripheral vision, I noticed a mass of angry white water on our port stern rapidly gaining ground on the Agivey.

Wallace returned to the deck and told me to keep the wheel while he secured items in the cockpit. By now Nanette had disappeared behind the headland sheltering Portnahaven. We were on our own and found the wireless was not functioning! I had lots of confidence in the Agivey having sailed with her for over 20 years in many circumstances. She doesn't like a beam sea but can ride out most seas if handled gently. There was nothing gentle about this sea however, as the direction kept changing with troughs opening on the port beam then the starboard, crests curving over the stern. The Agivey was towing the 12-foot Blue Boat dinghy on twin painters and suddenly she was no longer there. I was told afterwards the vision of her vertical on the face of a wave had terrified the crew in the cockpit who thought the little boat was heading for them.

This was Ashley's first experience of open sea sailing and all he could do was cling on and think the worst. Wallace said afterwards these were the worst conditions he had experienced in 70-years-plus. A fortune teller had told him that he would not die by drowning. But what about his crew! Having to wrestle with the wheel to keep the sea in the right quarter, I hadn't time to fully consider long term prospects, just edge the Agivey shoreward where the water appeared relatively calmer.

After an endless time, probably 20 to 30 minutes, we reached water calm enough to bring about and head southwards to round the headland. Behind it was the welcome sight of Nanette, at anchor off Portnahaven. A fisherman advised us to use one of the permanent buoys: the storm would make the anchorage insecure. The Rambler was storm bound on Islay for about a week, now we stayed in port until another tempest expired.

After the trauma of that first leg, the beauty of the Hebrides took over and we were as enchanted as the Rambler crew was. The majesty of Staffa and Mull, the serenity of Colonsay and Iona, and many idyllic bays made this a trip to remember. As usual with Wallace, the social aspect stands out. Meals on board and ashore, 'noon balloons', visitors planned and unplanned — these things always attracted me to sail with Wallace.

Ros writes:

Wallace was 'an old sailor' who believed the risk of being drowned at sea was an accepted entitlement for the elements in exchange for the thrills and excitements of being waterborne. Life jackets just prolonged the process.

I first joined him on Agivey in 1998 to start research for our 'Donegal Islands' book — refreshing his memories whilst introducing me to the Islands and their delights, which I then painted. Little did I realise what life on a boat was really like. From an early age I'd been on his different yachts for day outings or the odd two days at a time. I'd promised my partner Tim that I'd wear the nice neat life jacket he bought me — over the shoulders and tied round the waist. It automatically inflated if you fell in the water. On one occasion, we'd been out for half an hour when the shelter of the land no longer protected us, and we hit choppy waters. I went down to my cabin and put on the life jacket. When I emerged, three sets of eyes regarded me silently. I explained that I had promised. Then both fellow crewmen, Graham Kane and Ricky Butler, disappeared and came back with equivalent jackets and short smiles. "What about you Wallace?" I said. This was greeted with a dismissive grunt. However, a short time later he too disappeared, and after thumps and rummaging noises, he appeared wearing two huge orange squares of cork, forrard and aft, strapped around his large torso. "Useless," he said, but with a very puckish grin.

The only other time I ventured to mention a life jacket was on our Staffa voyage amongst the 'overfalls'. This time he emerged with an airline safety jacket. "Blow it up," I suggested. It was obvious after several puffs that nothing would happen, so it too was jettisoned. But in a small way this illustrates that Wallace, though set in his ways, was sensitive to other ideas, and could make concessions.

CHAPTER 13
A Sweet Adriatic Swansong
2010

Bruce:

When Wallace sold Agivey in 2009, it was the first time in 60 years that he lacked a boat of his own. He confided to friends that he found this loss very hard to accept. He would never be short of invitations to sail. But he missed being part of the fraternity of boat owners and skippers: that close-knit club of mariners who care so fondly for their vessels, and eagerly shoulder the countless small responsibilities that owning a boat involves. Inevitably, his home commitments, and his own stiffness and other infirmities, made it hard for him to get away to sea, even on borrowed craft. But he still yearned for the waves, and by summer 2010 he reckoned he should use whatever strength he had left for a final burst of sailing. Without telling many people, he made a plan to charter a boat off the coast of Croatia with three trusted sailing companions. This was indeed his last sea voyage, but the trip, in September 2010, was also one of the most enjoyable journeys of Wallace's later years.

A crucial participant in this venture was Des Moran, a wise doctor from Sligo who, despite being Wallace's junior by a couple of decades, had been a particularly close friend of late. Des and his wife Siobhan were outstandingly loyal to Wallace during his final months of infirmity, making the five-hour road journey from Sligo to Belfast with remarkable frequency, even in conditions of ice and snow. Des later combined a threnody for Wallace with a happy recollection of the sailing they had enjoyed in the Adriatic.

Des Moran:

When Wallace died on 8 May, 2011, our hearts' barometers fell and the mournful cry of curlews made full the evening air. On the day of his funeral, one heard words like courage, loyalty, generosity, leadership and friendship: all well used, and with great sincerity.

I remember visiting Wallace, Miles and the other crew when the Aileach galley anchored at Malinbeg harbour under mighty Slieve League. Wallace was skipper, and at 64 he slept out on the open boat. He outpaced his crew as they climbed up the steep steps of the harbour. As always, he met you with his thumb-dislocating *handshake. You knew where you stood with a man like that. His last cruise was in Croatia with a familiar team – Ricky Butler, Graham Kane and myself – in autumn 2010. He also had the great pleasure of sailing with his grandson Finnian who was travelling round Europe with his cousin Lydia... Wallace had a great gift for listening to young people, and being interested in what they had to say. He had that rare ability to make everyone feel important... and he always maintained the many friendships he formed in a remarkable life.*

This is how Wallace described the voyage:

I thought I had swallowed the hook for keeps after I sold *Agivey* in January and clocked up an 83rd birthday. I was no longer fit to 'hand, reef and steer' or even 'fit out, launch and lay up' as I had done each year for the last half century. This was it! Then arose a chance of one more sortie. There might be some kick in the old horse yet.

Des Moran, Ricky Butler and Graham Kane, the cream of *Agivey* hands, joined me to arrange charter of an Odessa 40 from Split. They are a bunch of seasoned skippers, navigators, nippy foredeck hands, powerful winch winders and above all good judges of food and drink! What more could a shipmate ask?

Admiralty charts now cost £20 apiece. Doesn't seem long since it was £2.50. For planning I bought Number 196 – Bar to Split which shows 20 islands and a wee bit of the Italian coast. There were handy small-sized Croatian charts on board but so well used that the old joke about the Cornish skipper plotting a course round Land's End applied: "If them's fly shit we'arl right. But if them's rocks we'm buggered." Actually, there are not a lot of offshore rocks here. Those that occur are well marked by lights and beacons.

We flew from Dublin to Zadar on 11 September. The town, or should I say City of Split, after a long drive appeared at midnight as blazing lights and a huge marina. Our Odessa 40 was just one of 30 similar boats due out with new crews next day. All the gear was there including nice fresh bedding – but no spinnaker or life raft. The inflatable dinghy proved leaky enough to guarantee wet bums on the shortest journey. Otherwise no complaints. The engine always started first bonk and ran like a quiet dream.

My cabin aft had less than one square yard of deck space and required some gymnastics to get feet under the cockpit, but once you were in, you were in! Good enough for the likes of me! My 20-year old grandson,

Finnian, and his cousin, Lydia, were rail-roading round Europe and had recently toured Vienna. I suggested by phone that they join us for a day or two on board. They made for Zagreb where they were shown round by a journalist friend. Now they were in a hostel in Split. Morning brought them backpacking along Catwalk Charlie to our berth and tripping up the steep narrow gangplank.

After introductions, coffee and the arrival of Graham bearing food for a week we slipped. A sunlit calm passage to Milna at the east end of Brac Island followed while we got to know the ropes. We found a berth alongside for a tasty cockpit lunch of *saucisson* and exotic fruits with a choice of red or white local wines and coffee strong enough to trot a mouse on. A little shopping then slipped again, just in time to avoid paying dues, for a return to Split.

The Croatian coast is said to contain 1,240 islands. Enough to appear as overlaps and super-impositions when the pinky blue silhouetted isles beckon across a shimmering blue sea from the mainland. On a small scale chart they look like elongated sausages or bulgy ovals. Closer up they have many inlets, often tortuous or hammer-headed, with pretty red-roofed villages and secluded anchorages tucked round the corners. There are no less than 32 marinas. Next day we had a five-hour run before an offshore wind. Finn and Lydia took turns at the helm. In this ship, as Francis Drake put it a few years back, "the gentlemen hauled and drew with the mariners." So they quickly learned to trim sheets then sunbathed on the foredeck.

Next day our call was Bisevo, a satellite of Vis. Des out-boarded us by turn into The Blue Grotto. You pay a boatman outside, duck under the entrance and proceed about 50 feet straight inwards in pitch darkness. Then a low starboard tunnel leads into The Grand Chambre. This is lit from the bottom by sunlight reflected as a pale green glow off the flat sandy floor. Slightly spooky like the Greek Entrance to Hades in the Peloponese. Bigger than the more famous Capri Grotto. No less than 12 yacht crews queued up behind us to enter. Signs of abandoned light cables mark unsuccessful efforts to use artificial illumination. It is best visited around midday when the sun shines direct into the entrance. (In northeast Antrim we have a dozen sea caves more lovely by far. Perhaps they could be developed for public viewing. They were popular 50 years ago. Giant's Causeway fishermen used to row boatfuls of viewers in and out.)

We spent the night in Komica, stern to the pier; this is at the west end of

Vis. Finn and Lydia departed on the hired bikes we'd brought along on board... an unusual deck cargo. They were due in Italy 36 hours later and faced a stiff pull over the 1,500-foot mountainous crest. We would all miss their cheery presence.

Our friend Tim had told us about a family living on a tiny star-shaped islet just east of Vis. Their cuisine is far famed – cooked by request and only if they like you. After a morning's slow sail a pleasant anchorage off the landing sheltered by reefs and islets seemed welcoming. *Hello Dolie* (*sic*) was already in. Glimpses of a small house could be seen through a fringe of twisted maritime pine. We entrusted to Des the delicate task of securing the approval of Mine Host. The latter said, 'No can do' at first, but when told we had come all the way from the 'Land of Saints and Dollars', especially to taste his fare, he said he might go fishing and see what he caught. "Come back about seven and we'll see."

We landed on small white stones and ascended 50 feet by rough steps. The pleasantest of dinners followed. A small bass each and a bigger longer-shaped one to share were shown to us first then grilled over wood on a massive open air stone. Wines from a local vineyard were served at a long trestle table in a veranda in front of the house. Through tree trunks we could see the Adriatic, calm blue in the lee of the island, wimpled by breeze further out. A gibbous moon lit the scene.

Next day it was a longish leg to Otak Hvar – *otak* meaning island. How is your Serbo-Croatian? Ours was improving. We knew three words now! Including *otak*, there was *hvala* (which I pronounced koala) for thank you and *luka* for port or harbour. But we were pale creatures with our untanned legs and torsos, and perhaps for that reason did not get many second glances.

A mention of the nudist colony in Hvar got the crew's attention. Hvar was the ancient capital of the Isles and her shores were sea-whitened limestone at sea level – you could tell the degree of exposure to the swell by the width of the white band; the same rock appeared grey between shrubberies higher up. Narrow roads and trails could barely be made out among the dark trees. There must be iron oxide about to create the powerful magnetic anomalies which made the compass whirl. But mostly we steered by eye or by the traditional shathmont which gives a bearing of so many degrees from fingers of an extended hand.

Our berth was in a marina as usual. I can't say I like marinas, although they have their uses. Here one often has no choice. A bit further north we entered canyon-like channels and lakes extending many miles inland, passing under fine lofty bridges to the National Park of Krk (pronounced with a click from half-way down your throat). There were six yachts ahead of us, four more astern as we motored between 200-foot cliffs. Buoys marking fish farms lined each side for the first mile or two. This is a unique seaway, widening into lakes at intervals. Everyone was most friendly. All boats gave smiling waves *en passant* and were ready to help with mooring, so it wasn't just *faux bonhomie*. Their gleaming white sails appeared immaculate and were smartly handled. But hulls tend to be ugly, with little or no sheer, looking as if built by the mile and cut off in fifty-foot lengths – bows either vertical or pointed with all the finesse of a Stanley knife blade. They were mostly big'uns, anything under 50 feet counting as small fry. I missed my dear old 35-foot *Wild Goose* and Ricky his beautifully kept early Caribee, Number 35.

We entered the top marina 14 miles from the sea between a pair of 30-foot gilded bird's wings. Ricky was expert at making accurate stern boards, sometimes in cross winds, between packed angular hulls – a tricky job. He never touched the wrong spot. Not once. A little help came from the way that our Odessa showed little or no tendency to kick to one side or other when going astern – perhaps because of the gap between the propeller and rudder.

Graham at the bow infallibly caught up the head mooring with the wobbly boathook – it would have served well in a dinghy – and made fast on a pair of cleats. We kept the Bimini overhead all the time – the sun at midday was a little strong. Even the smallest local boats had some overhead protection. Big 'cattle boats', as New Englanders call passenger cruisers, were always in sight, with varnished wooden upper works over white plastic hulls. Some had steved-up bowsprits for added effect.

Next day we took a motor boat up river to see the Falls. The water taxi was free, but a peep at the Falls cost money. They were worth it. Descending 150 feet in several steps, they were not as big as Niagara but much better than the Swallow Falls in Wales and were surrounded by attractive woodland and much frothy foam.

We went down stream in the afternoon, then due west – a relief to be in open sea – to a wooded island where we found a V-shaped bay with no signs of recent habitation and a convenient ten fathoms for anchoring. Many inter-island soundings are very deep. Each side of our cove was clad in pine, plane and cypress trees. A surly crew came in about 2200 and anchored at the inner apex, so didn't disturb our peace. They flew a German ensign. Their boat was an old time wooden cutter, about eight tons, with a lovely sheer and a curving bow that might have come off a Herreshoff drawing board – far the best looker we saw on the whole trip!

A couple of nights alongside at Rogac on Solta Island followed. A hundred houses fringed the bay with small boats stern-to all round. A large wooden cross showed the affiliations of the inhabitants. One very old house was roofed with rough white stones, a pleasant change from the universal brick red tiles. There were no harbour dues on the east side where the big ferries berth. Instead there were cats – black cats, white cats, brown cats, tawny cats, parked on the stones of the pier beside us ready to leap on board at the sign of a fish tail – too well fed to eat mere bread and butter. We dined well ashore at sea level across the harbour – the cats followed – and I recall especially tasty steak, risotto and island wines with pleasure.

We were almost expecting loud hails of, 'Come in number nine, your time is up!' but had one more exquisite day, sailing round to the west side to a rocky creek labelled R1 on the Admiralty Chart, and there to anchor, bathe and lunch in deep water seclusion. Dinner on board later was eating up all that was left of Graham's carefully worked out rations.

It blew and rained hard on our way east to Split in the morning, but that was the only bad weather of the fortnight. From our homes in the Six Counties to Dublin airport, three hours flying then more motoring to Split had been a wearisome 14-hour journey. Same going back. It would have been quicker getting to the USA! But many thanks to my shipmates for helping hands when I looked like wobbling off the narrow gangplanks.

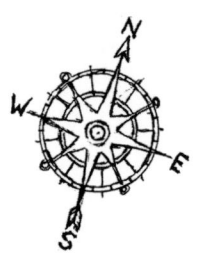

'Sea-Fever' by John Masefield

I must go down to the seas again, to the lonely sea and the sky,
And all I ask is a tall ship and a star to steer her by,
And the wheel's kick and the wind's song and the white sail's shaking,
And a grey mist on the sea's face and a grey dawn breaking.

I must go down to the seas again, for the call of the running tide
Is a wild call and a clear call that may not be denied;
And all I ask is a windy day with the white clouds flying,
And the flung spray and the blown spume, and the sea-gulls crying.

I must go down to the seas again to the vagrant gypsy life,
To the gull's way and the whale's way where the wind's like a whetted knife;
And all I ask is a merry yarn from a laughing fellow-rover,
And quiet sleep and a sweet dream when the long trick's over.

Extract from the Irish Cruising Club obituary
by W M Nixon

Wallace Clark, a member since 1951 and our Commodore from 1960 to 1963, brought a breath of fresh air to a club which had formerly been almost exclusively linked to Ireland's main sailing centres. He didn't come from a family with any direct sailing traditions or maritime connections at all. Some parts of his life, such as a career in the linen business at the family's mills in the relatively remote village of Upperlands, were pre-ordained. But his passion for the sea was more mysterious. His maternal kin, the Stuarts, included a couple of Admirals. But neither parent, nor any other immediate forebear, was any sort of sailing enthusiast, let alone one who aspired to cruise in small boats. Yet from boyhood he was determined to get afloat. Initially this was on the limited sailing water provided by the dams around the linen mill, which had been in business since the 1730s.

The nearest sea to Upperlands was Ireland's rugged north coast, and the even more challenging northwestern seaboard. But by 1950 he was regularly sailing these north and northwest coasts in his own small three-tonner, covering more than a thousand miles in all. At that time, neither coasts had significant sailing activity, thus every venture had an element of exploration to it, and he began accumulating the local knowledge which was to make his later work in the area of sailing directions and local history so useful to fellow-sailors.

Portrush was nominally his home port, but he developed a lifelong ability to select suitable mooring locations where the boat could be safely left at the end of a weekend cruise, rather than being restricted to returning to the home port. It was an essential skill long before the era of visitor's moorings or strategically-located marinas, and it added to his already extensive range of friends and acquaintances living along the coast, for much as he enjoyed long periods afloat with little company, ashore he was gregarious, providing entertaining and increasingly erudite company.

With the energy of youth, he cheerfully disregarded the fearful reputation of Ireland's Atlantic coastline among the Northern Ireland cruising establishment (they almost invariably cruised in the accessible and sheltered Hebrides), and set off in 1951, in *Zamorin*, to sail round Ireland in this small craft no longer in her prime of life. Visiting yachts were an extreme rarity on Ireland's west coast in those days, so the young crew made a formidable impact in the anchorages and islands they visited, and for their skipper it was the beginning of an enduring enthusiasm for Europe's most remote coastline.

When they reached the south coast and sailed into Cork Harbour, they were welcomed as heroes, and *Zamorin's* crew in turn were impressed by the high level of sailing activity – both racing and cruising – which was an integral part of life in Cork. The Crosshaven welcome reinforced his growing involvement with the Irish Cruising Club. He had been elected a member at the beginning of the year on the strength of his cruises with the three-tonner, and his remarkable 1951 circumnavigation of Ireland was marked with the award (you don't 'win' cruising trophies) of the Faulkner Cup.

However, the cruise had revealed *Zamorin's* limitations, and by May 1952 he'd bought *Caru*, a good-looking and much more modern McGruer-designed Bermudan sloop, built in 1938. He wasted no time in utilising this performance, with a 1,380 mile cruise from Portrush to Brittany and back. His achievements with this able little slip of a boat were prodigious – in 1953 he took her to Norway, and then in 1954 he made his second round Ireland cruise, receiving the Round Ireland Cup, and adding to the experiences which would eventually become his seminal book, 'Sailing Round Ireland', which was to be published, after further extensive cruising on the Irish coast, in 1976.

He was also a frequent sailing visitor to the Scottish west coast and islands, in time building up an intimate knowledge of that complex cruising area which was to be rivalled only by his knowledge of the Irish coast. That Irish insight was being put to good use with his considerable active input into the developing coverage of the Irish Cruising Club's two volumes of 'Sailing Directions', which in time would cover the entire coastline in regularly up-dated detail, an achievement in which Wallace Clark's contribution was unrivalled.

He was also active in the ICC's administration, joining the committee in the 1950s, and ascending the officer ladder by becoming Rear Commodore in 1956, Vice Commodore in 1958, and the Club's most youthful Commodore in 1960, just nine years after becoming a member, the first Commodore from the north. He led by example. By this time he had moved up in boat size to the 36-foot Bermudan yawl *Wild Goose*.

She was the yacht with which Wallace Clark was to be most intimately associated. He was by now married to June and with a young family. But instead of this limiting his sailing, he showed what could be done with energy and imagination by the careful selection of cruising areas which could accommodate all family levels of enthusiasm and ability, while at the same time feeding his own delight in remote islands and hidden anchorages. The west coasts of Ireland and Scotland provided endless opportunities, and so too did Brittany, but as well for a period during the 1960s he based his boat in the Mediterranean and brought a fresh eye with his writings on coasts and islands far from his usual home port.

At the same time, his interest in the history of ancient boat types used in the narrow but often rough waters between Ireland and the nearest Scottish islands was continuing to develop, and in 1963 he played a central role and was the sailing master for a re-creation on its 400th anniversary of the voyage from Derry to Iona by St Columba, using a 30-foot sailing curragh built in Donegal. Later, his unique experience in sailing large curraghs led to his being a crew member for part of the *Brendan* voyage of Tim Severin in 1976, while his fascination with the boats of the Celtic seaways was carried a stage further with the building of the Lord of the Isles galley *Aileach*, based on a mediaeval general purpose sailing vessel depicted in a stone carving at Rodel in the Outer Hebrides, which was re-created by boatbuilders at Greencastle in Donegal, and sailed under Clark's command from Galway to the Western Isles and Stornoway.

His attractive writing style became more widely known through magazine outlets and several books. A convivial shipmate, he much enjoyed the gatherings – particularly the informal and spontaneous ones – which a shared love of sailing the sea inspired.

Sustained by many friends from ashore and afloat, his zest for life continued despite personal setbacks which might have dismayed a lesser man. However, time took its toll, and in January 2010 aged 83, he felt it was time to sell *Agivey* and become boatless for the first time in 70 years. But there were still opportunities for sailing, and during the summer of 2010 he wrote with delight of cruising with three old shipmates – Des Moran ICC, Ricky Butler ICC, and Graham Kane – on a chartered yacht in Croatia, joined for a few days by his grandson Finnian.

The account of this sun-drenched cruise in the 2010 annual is classic Wallace Clark – insights into local history and nautical habits, interspersed with the frequent conveyance of a sense of enjoyment, and filled with useful information for fellow sailors. He concluded: "Best thanks to my shipmates for helping hands when I looked like wobbling off those narrow gangplanks, and support all along. We hadn't seen a newspaper or watched TV for a fortnight. Hope we'll manage to go again."

It was not to be. He was knocked down by a truck while walking near his home, and despite an heroic struggle against many painful injuries, he died in early May 2011 aged 84. He has left an extraordinary legacy of historical and maritime interest, all infused with his own unique character. Wallace Clark is much mourned in many areas of life.

Meet the Fleet

'Ships are all right. It's the men in'em.'
Uffa Fox (Boat designer & sailing enthusiast)

Spluto
10-foot punt. The Clark children's first boat.

Falcon
12-foot clinker sailing dinghy. Used up and down the River Bann.

The Whaler
17-foot open double-ender dipping lug. Clinker built with four wide planks aside. Bought by Alec Cooke in Stavanger, Norway. Shipped home, leaving Hamburg in September 1939, two days ahead of the outbreak of World War II. Mainly used for Rock Pigeon shooting and fishing. Trips included Culdaff and Kintyre.

San Ferian
18-foot half-decker, Gunter rig. Carvel-built in Portrush by Billy Lee, 1946. Shared with cousin, Roland Clark.

Fugitive
21-foot, three-ton inshore racer; Belfast Lough No 2 Class sloop. Built ca 1900.

Zamorin
25-foot, seven-ton TM Loch Fyne Skiff. Gaff cutter Rig. Built by Hilditch, Carrickfergus ca 1898. Bought for £450 plus £15 for tender. 1951 round Ireland trip – 'Round Ireland in Zamorin' was the author's first Irish Cruising Club log publication, and Wallace was awarded the 1951 ICC Faulkner Cup for this trip.

Caru
27-foot, five-ton TM Auxiliary Bermudan Sloop. Built on the Clyde by James McGruer for Glasgow Exhibition, 1938. 1952 Brittany (1st trip to France) – won Cruising Association Hanson Cup; 1953 Norway – won Cruising Association Love Cup; 1954 round Ireland – awarded Irish Cruising Club Navigation Cup.

Wild Goose
35-foot, ten-ton Bermudan yawl. Built by Kings of Pin Mill, 1935.

Designed by Maurice Griffiths. Bought from Mervyn Henry of Coleraine, 1955 and sailed extensively until her sinking in 1998 at the Barmouth. (Subsequently restored by Robin Ruddock.)

Agivey
Fibre Glass 32-foot Colvic Atlantic Ketch ca. 1970. Acquired a one-third share in 1999, took sole ownership in 2007, and sold her in 2009.

The Nine Lives of 'Wild Goose'

W*ild Goose* remained a lucky boat for me in spite of the rechristening. However, it was perhaps thanks to her original owner naming her *Wild Lone II*, the name of Rudyard Kipling's feline in his poem 'The Cat That Walked by Herself', that she appeared to be blessed with the nine lives of a cat, as she was tested to the cruising limits.

~ Life 1 – Failed Mooring ~
The first cat's life was used up in 1956, three days before I was due to get married. In the gale that often blows fiercely at the end of August, our moorings in Portrush harbour gave way (we used to lay our own in those days). Instead of getting severely battered on rock walls to leeward, *Wild Goose* brought up gently on a narrow strand of beach.

~ Life 2 – On The Wrong Course ~
The next escape came years later after leaving Dún Laoghaire at dusk bound for Brittany. Harry, a trusty helmsman in daylight, found it difficult to see the compass at night and unwittingly steered four points off course.

Dozing below, the first I knew that she was in trouble was when horrifying judders were heard as we struck the bottom. We were supposed to be five miles offshore, but Harry had landed us on the outer edge of the Arklow Bank, a known ship's graveyard. We were on a falling tide and our chances seemed slim but after a dozen bumps *Wild Goose's* luck brought her off and she was undamaged. Just a year before a 40-foot ketch hit the same bank and sank!

~ Life 3 – Into The Breakers ~
My wife, June, and I were anchored just north of Scalasaigs on Tiree. The bay is shallow and open to the east, so when it blew up from this direction at dawn, we decided to get out. The nearest shelter was in Gunna Sound between Tiree and Coll. June was at the tiller and the waves were building

up. I was looking at the shoreline for a place where we could shelter close in when June suddenly yelled, "Breakers ahead!" A low reef, not shown clearly on our much used fathom chart was now just awash. June's quick 'hard to starboard' seemed to clear it but our iron keel struck on the hidden outer end. We bounced and slithered over. A few minutes later we had the anchor down in calm water.

~ Life 4 – Lee Shore ~

One gusty November weekend we sailed from Portrush to Rathlin and anchored in a small bay on the east side. The forecast was westerly and we seemed snug enough but laid out an anchor to seaward to be on the safe side. It was as well we did – the grumble of the swell on the rocks around us rose steadily during the long autumn night.

A dirty dawn revealed the wind blowing a steady Force 5 from the east. We had already dragged a bit and were snubbing on the seaward anchor with our stern a length from the island. 'Get out quick!' was the answer but there was a lot of foredeck work to do, with two anchor warps and 50m of chain to come in. Luckily Mike Villiers-Stuart, a square-rig man with the strength of a tiger and nerves of steel, was on the bow. Somehow he got the warps and chain on deck, allowing us to sail out. Half an hour later the gusts coming off Fair Head touched Force 9 and we gybed so fiercely that the boom kicked up and jammed on the backstay. However, *Wild Goose* shrugged it off and saw us safely on our way south.

~ Life 5 – Fire Down Below ~

The same Mike in a Midi Canal Lock on the way to the Med promised us a rum omelette to celebrate his birthday. It flambéed high and ignited the curtains. We had a job to stop the lock-keeper putting his fire hose on us to douse the smoke!

~ Life 6 – Snapped Anchor Chain ~

Wild Goose had another narrow escape off Greencastle at the mouth of Lough Foyle when my friend Paul Campbell anchored her at the entrance to the harbour, which was then much smaller than it is today. The dawn wind gusted up sharp from the SE, the worst possible quarter. She was snubbing hard as Paul eyed the situation anxiously. Suddenly, the three-eighths chain snapped. Only smart work with engine and sails got her clear of rocks a boat's length to leeward. The scope was short and when she kicked her bow up, there was nothing to absorb the shock.

~ Life 7 – Navigational Error ~

The entrance to the River Bann in County Derry, Ireland, known as the Barmouth, has a pair of training walls extending 200m seawards from a lengthy beach. In 1985, my son Miles was returning from Scotland in the dark and made the mistake of taking the west training wall on the wrong side, getting dangerously close to the beach at Castlerock. The lift of the ground swell warned him and he was able to get her turned round and out to sea.

~ Life 8 – Near Collision ~

An escape from collision came on the River Volga in Russia when Miles was heading south from the White to Black Sea in 1994. Miles and his Russian crew, Nikolai, had just left the lock at Gorodets when a big steel ship appeared round the next bend. Nikolai, on the tiller, took appropriate action by putting her head to starboard when a 'honk' from astern indicated that a tanker was about to overtake from his starboard quarter. There was plenty of room for three ships in the river but at the last minute a dredger that had been working alongshore to port hauled out from the bank. This forced the tanker into the middle of the river. *Wild Goose* was trapped between walls of steel no more than 20-feet apart and seemed bound to be crushed as they raced passed. It was all over in less than a minute and probably the prop wash from the first steamer, which was flying light with no cargo, pushed *Wild Goose* clear. Nikolai breathed a hearty sigh of relief when they came clear and remarked, "Anything is possible for a good Bolshevik!"

~ Life 9 – Sunk In Sight Of Home ~

One dark, gusty night in 1998 it was me who dropped a real clanger at the Barmouth. Four rows of salmon nets, spread close to seaward of the mouth of the River Bann forced us to approach from the east close inshore. Our bow lookout said, "Turn in now." I still blush with shame at mistaking the east wall ahead for the west with its light beacon, which we should have had on our starboard hand to enter. I put the tiller up and by the time the beach surf loomed through the dark it was too late to get her head round. We grounded and grinded on our bilge among small breakers. The first wave over the stern had knocked out our 12v electrical system, and with it the VHF radio. It was a call on a mobile phone that brought the Coastguard along a mile of beach in their Land Rover. The only thing to do was launch the liferaft and abandon ship. Then the Portrush lifeboat arrived and in shallow water and cross tides got a line onto *Wild Goose's* stern and towed her off. But the joy was short lived, *Wild Goose* took a big drink over her low counter and sank in 30-foot. If you are going to make a real ass of yourself there are few better places to do it than five miles from your home port.

There was a happy ending as my insurance company was very understanding and we were able to give *Wild Goose* to the Causeway Coast Maritime Heritage Group. Outdoor education instructor, Robin Ruddick, bought *Wild Goose* in 1999 from the CCMHG. The boat had spent a month on the seabed and the CCMHG found, once she was salvaged, they could not afford to restore her. Robin restored her over two years and now regularly sails her with his family to the Western Isles.

Lessons of a Lifetime's Cruising

The lessons are many: regular maintenance of moorings; not going to sea in bad weather; choosing anchor chain a size bigger than that recommended and always making sure to use the Log, Lead and Lookout system of sailing. We never had GPS, or echosounder.

But even taking all reasonable precautions, you still need a slice of luck – and owning a lucky boat is the best way to get it. In 1957, I myself appeared to have more than one life, when *Wild Goose* saved me from what seemed certain drowning on a return voyage from Brittany. We had left Audierne in a southwesterly gale under pressure to get back to work. I took over the tiller in tide-torn seas off Ouessant and was just fastening my safety harness when an unseen breaking crest hurled me out of the cockpit and over the lee side.

Boats of *Wild Goose's* vintage didn't have life-lines. Luckily I dragged the tiller to leeward with me – it was the only thing to hold on to – and this put her head round quickly on the other tack so that she hove-to. I was clinging with fingernails to the bulwark and had just said a mental goodbye when the old *Goose* did a half roll and seemed to scoop me back on board. It was one of the many times that I blessed her low freeboard aft. Year after year, *Wild Goose* reached her chosen cruising grounds around Ireland, across Scotland, south to Brittany and across Russia, safely.

Maurice, you did a fine and enduring job in creating a ship you described to me as 'a good long'un.' Thank you!

Post-voyage Hazes of the Brain
Hebridean Highlights

Voyage descriptions commonly cover planning, preparation, landfall, fun at the far end, new friendships and departure for home. The brain haze that hovers in the back of one's mind afterwards can be an additional pleasure. Here is the set of impressions that contribute to such a brain haze that I pencilled in the back of the log book while being driven home after a three-week cruise in the Hebrides:

~ *The first heave of the bow as it lifted to a swell outside the harbour heads.*

~ *Islets seen up-sun, floating over quicksilver waters.*

~ *Faraway blue mountains, viewed over dappled seas.*

~ *Eileen Casteil in the Treshnish silhouetted against a wall-to-wall sunset of colours as fierce as the inside of a blast furnace.*

~ *Skye seen as mighty, black hills rising against the far off light.*

~ *Fog wraiths 500-feet deep, blanking off the bottom of the 1,000-foot cliffs close by.*

~ *Barra's peak in the distance, temptingly on the skyline under a ceiling of grey cloud.*

~ *A lonely buoy off Scalpay, tilting in the swell and showing its red underbody through translucent water. Tidal whirlpools plucking at the tiller in narrows between Skye and Raasay.*

~ *A brave male merganser flying tight circles over his mate to drive off predatory gulls as she swam ahead of her chicks – reminiscent of an aircraft carrier flying a Combat Air Patrol.*

~ *'Father and Child' – a male guillemot swimming two miles off the land with a half-grown chick beside him.*

~ *A coronet of cormorants perched on a low arching reef.*

~ *Lying at ease, chin over the rail, to watch the bow pushing ripples over still water and throwing ahead tiny bubbles to be eaten up by the advancing wave which begot them.*

~ *Two pairs of dolphins leaping joyfully alongside the bow for almost an hour off Coll.*

~ *Sounds that contribute to the brain haze include the rattle of an anchor chain; the tap of halliards against a wooden mast; the flutter of the leach of a sail when close hauled; the sucking dry of a bilge pump; the kettle boiling below for early morning tea; gulls croaking in a weird chorus and seals moaning out of sight in the dusk. Best of all, the sound of clinking glass as a 'noon balloon' is handed up on a tray to the cockpit. All these auditory delights help minimise shore cares; business, domestic or social obligations temporarily shrink to insignificance, as if seen from the wrong end of a telescope.*

~ *Sometimes in an anchorage it's a combination of different colours and surfaces that especially please. Tidal water swirling past slate rock contrasts the mobile with the static, the heather blooms shaking in a breeze above further highlighting and adding to the aesthetic visual mix.*

~ *The Middle Watch — our own navigation lights glowing softly on the sails and side decks.*

~ *At dawn — an eye-shaped patch of blue in an otherwise overcast sky. Is that God taking a look at us sailors below?*

~ *At the start of sunset — pools of pale blue with the smallest of white clouds, like a squashed archipelago of silvery islets, over the black hills of Jura.*

~ *Sailing south from Port Ellen — high pink cumulus over Ireland ahead.*

~ *The neat ellipse of Knocklayd Mountain showing over Rathlin's Altacarry lighthouse at the island's lowest end, with The Paps of Jura hidden in dark thunder clouds astern.*

~ *And, from dusk, the four flashes repeated every minute from Altacarry Head; the single red flash from The Bull.*

~ *An empty sea bar one distant coaster sighted during the passage to Ireland — about average for a crossing in the 21st century.*

Brain hazes like the above can extend a cruise and its pleasure by staying at the back of the mind for days, some for many weeks even. You could also say that a brain haze can hinder slotting back into every day life. While on board my brain relaxes and can lay off a course or pick a passage through rocks, 'strumbles' or tidal whirls, but it is useless for the first 24 hours ashore tackling business decisions or domestic dilemmas. And even as we drive the 20 miles home on the day of our return, eyes that have become used to looking only at far off views are irritated now by having to focus on multiple nearby hedges and house fronts. The green Irish countryside seems dull. Why? Because it is still, not moving as the sea constantly does. Seen from a boat, the sea is a living thing, always in motion, changing with the light, the wind and the action of the tide. In the same way as a tree or shrub becomes much more eye-catching and attractive when stirred by a breeze — it is the constant change, the poetry of motion that is a large part of the sea's charm. In conclusion, the oggin gives health, a chance of adventure, creates more friendships than any other element, and the brain hazes it creates are an important part of a priceless storehouse of memories.

Index